OMAHA BEACH ON D-DAY

PHOTOGRAPHS **Robert Capa**
STORY **Jean-David Morvan & Séverine Tréfouël**
DESIGN **Dominique Bertail**
ORIGINAL TEXT **Bernard Lebrun**
ENGLISH TRANSLATION **Edward Gauvin**

:01

First Second

NEW YORK

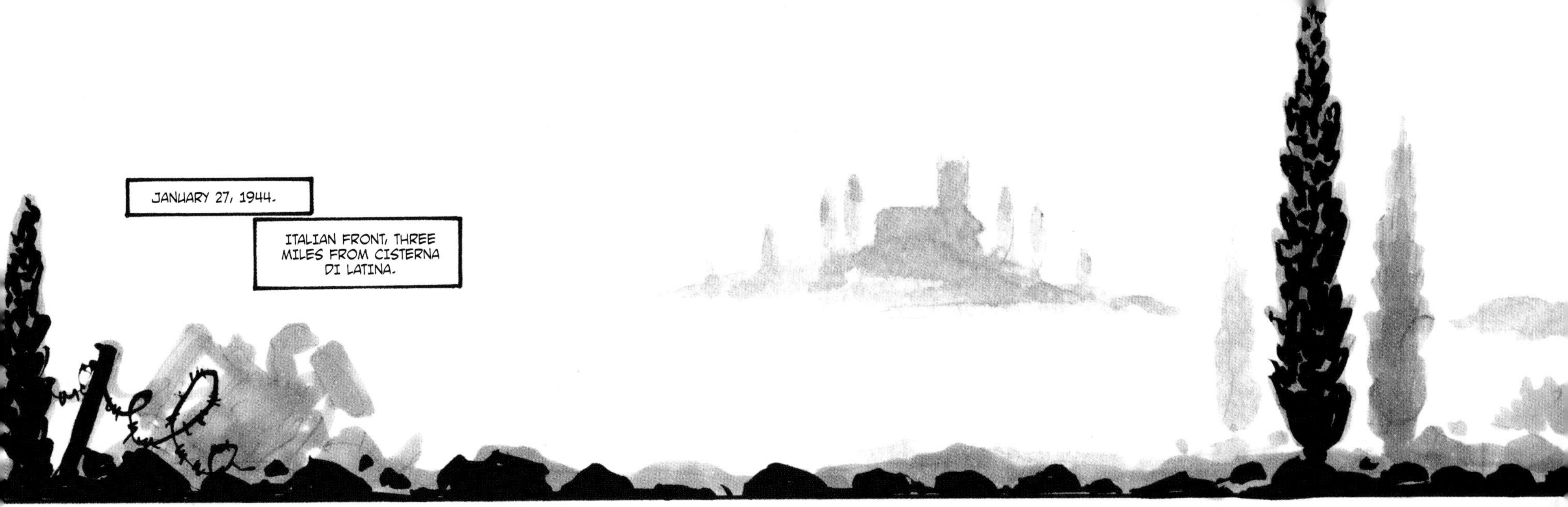
JANUARY 27, 1944.
ITALIAN FRONT, THREE MILES FROM CISTERNA DI LATINA.

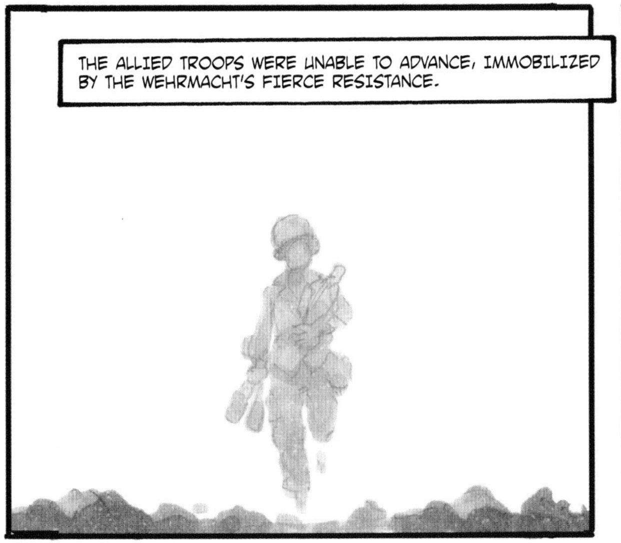
THE ALLIED TROOPS WERE UNABLE TO ADVANCE, IMMOBILIZED BY THE WEHRMACHT'S FIERCE RESISTANCE.

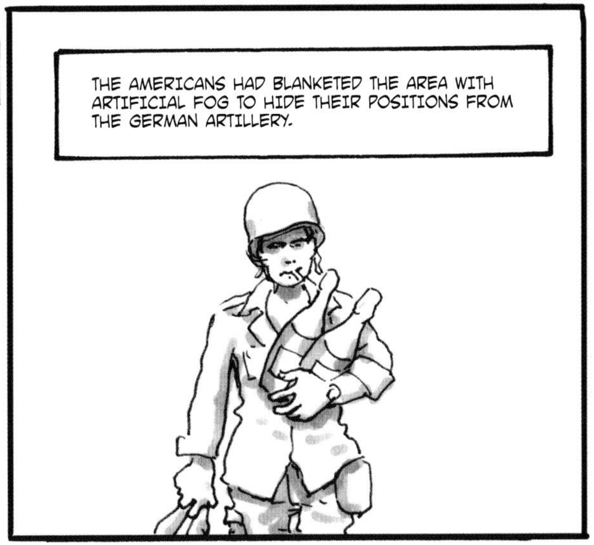
THE AMERICANS HAD BLANKETED THE AREA WITH ARTIFICIAL FOG TO HIDE THEIR POSITIONS FROM THE GERMAN ARTILLERY.

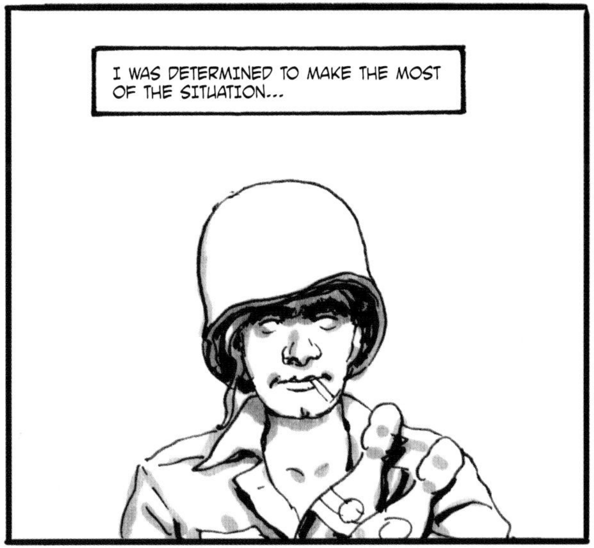
I WAS DETERMINED TO MAKE THE MOST OF THE SITUATION...

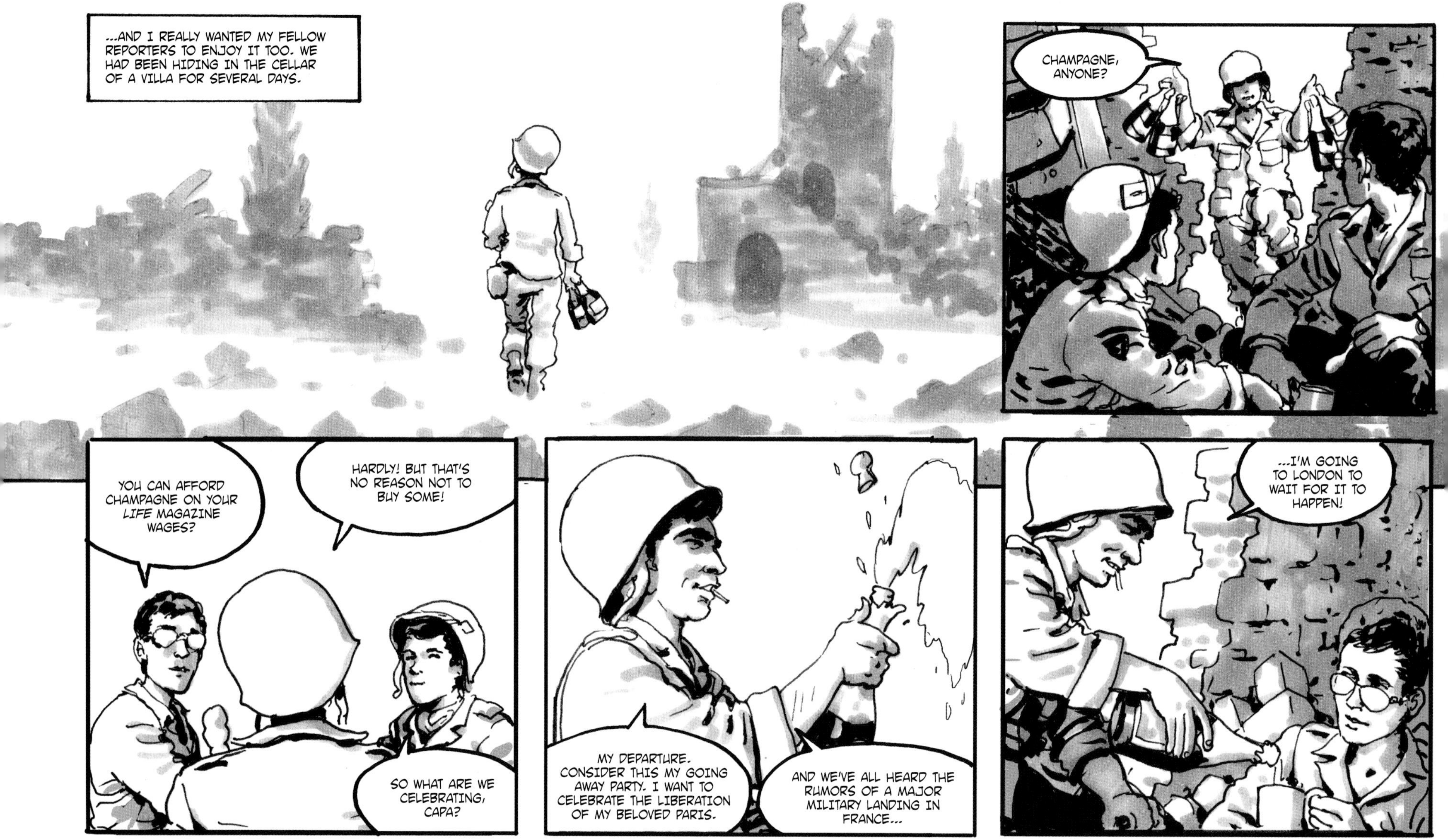
...AND I REALLY WANTED MY FELLOW REPORTERS TO ENJOY IT TOO. WE HAD BEEN HIDING IN THE CELLAR OF A VILLA FOR SEVERAL DAYS.
CHAMPAGNE, ANYONE?
YOU CAN AFFORD CHAMPAGNE ON YOUR *LIFE* MAGAZINE WAGES?
HARDLY! BUT THAT'S NO REASON NOT TO BUY SOME!
SO WHAT ARE WE CELEBRATING, CAPA?
MY DEPARTURE. CONSIDER THIS MY GOING AWAY PARTY. I WANT TO CELEBRATE THE LIBERATION OF MY BELOVED PARIS.
AND WE'VE ALL HEARD THE RUMORS OF A MAJOR MILITARY LANDING IN FRANCE...
...I'M GOING TO LONDON TO WAIT FOR IT TO HAPPEN!

MAY 22, 1944.
A MILITARY CLUB IN THE CENTER OF LONDON.

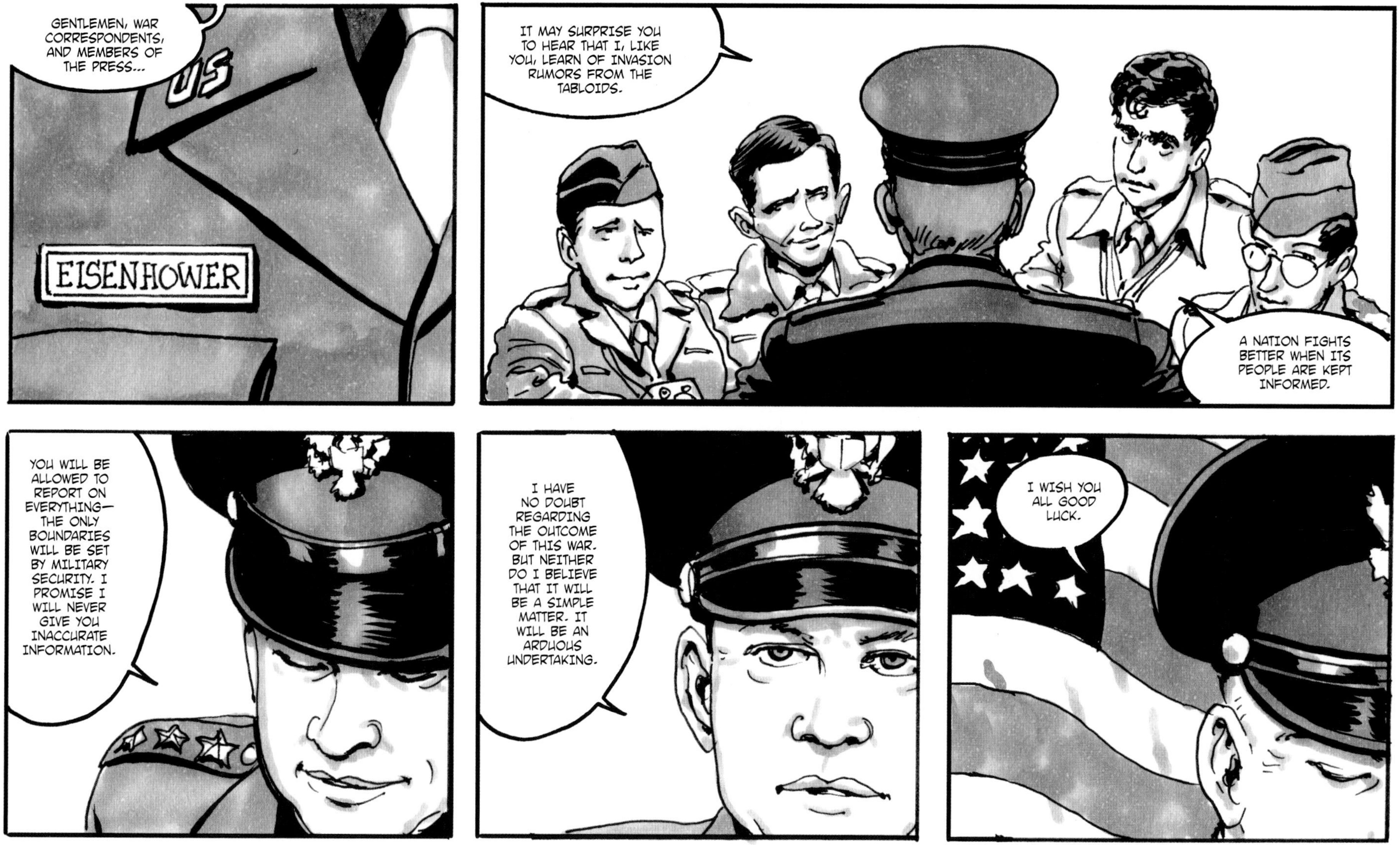
GENTLEMEN, WAR CORRESPONDENTS, AND MEMBERS OF THE PRESS...
US
EISENHOWER
IT MAY SURPRISE YOU TO HEAR THAT I, LIKE YOU, LEARN OF INVASION RUMORS FROM THE TABLOIDS.
A NATION FIGHTS BETTER WHEN ITS PEOPLE ARE KEPT INFORMED.
YOU WILL BE ALLOWED TO REPORT ON EVERYTHING—THE ONLY BOUNDARIES WILL BE SET BY MILITARY SECURITY. I PROMISE I WILL NEVER GIVE YOU INACCURATE INFORMATION.
I HAVE NO DOUBT REGARDING THE OUTCOME OF THIS WAR. BUT NEITHER DO I BELIEVE THAT IT WILL BE A SIMPLE MATTER. IT WILL BE AN ARDUOUS UNDERTAKING.
I WISH YOU ALL GOOD LUCK.

MAY 24, 1944. 26 LOWNDES SQUARE, LONDON.

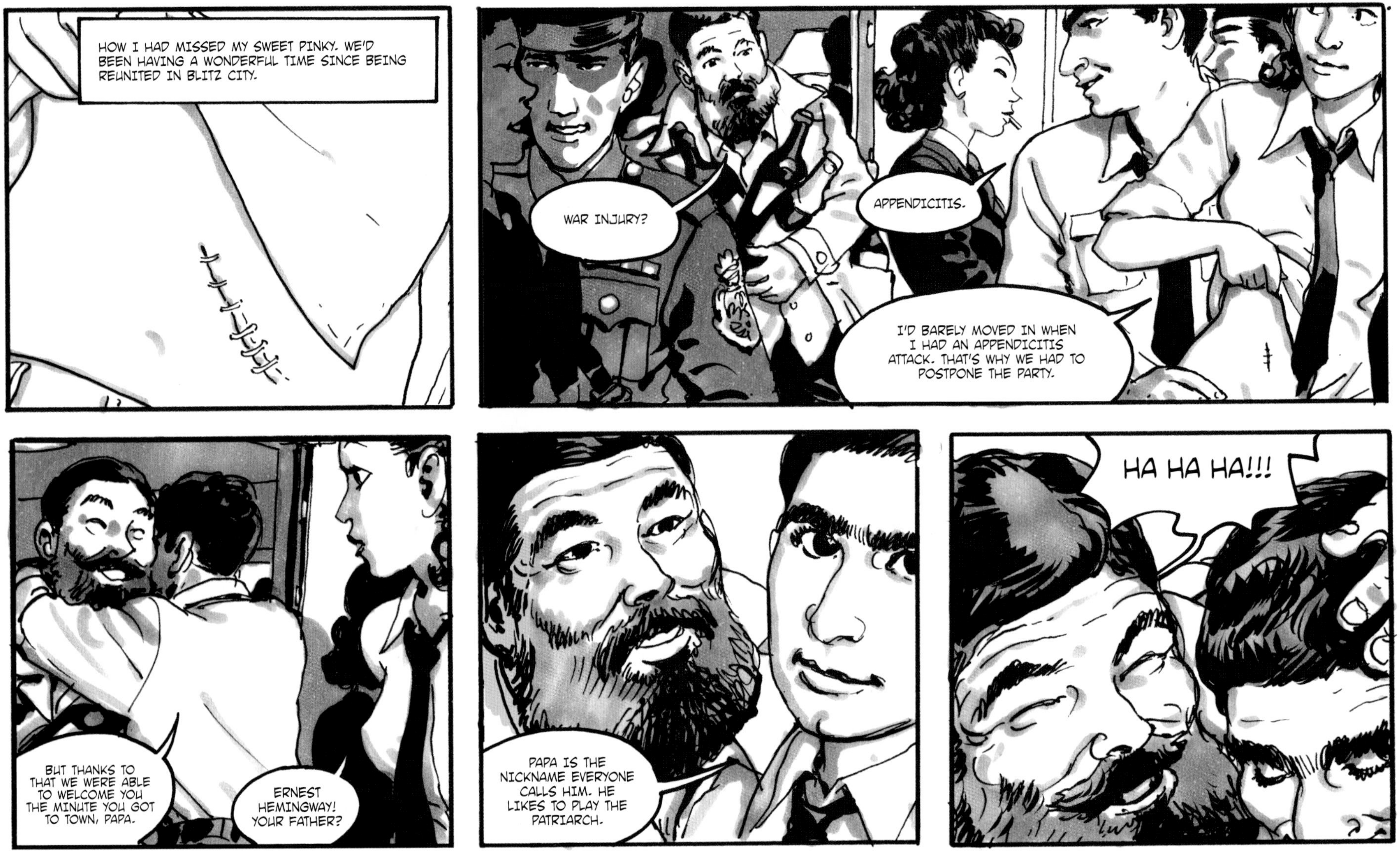

HOW I HAD MISSED MY SWEET PINKY. WE'D BEEN HAVING A WONDERFUL TIME SINCE BEING REUNITED IN BLITZ CITY.
WAR INJURY?
APPENDICITIS.
I'D BARELY MOVED IN WHEN I HAD AN APPENDICITIS ATTACK. THAT'S WHY WE HAD TO POSTPONE THE PARTY.
BUT THANKS TO THAT WE WERE ABLE TO WELCOME YOU THE MINUTE YOU GOT TO TOWN, PAPA.
ERNEST HEMINGWAY! YOUR FATHER?
PAPA IS THE NICKNAME EVERYONE CALLS HIM. HE LIKES TO PLAY THE PATRIARCH.
HA HA HA!!!

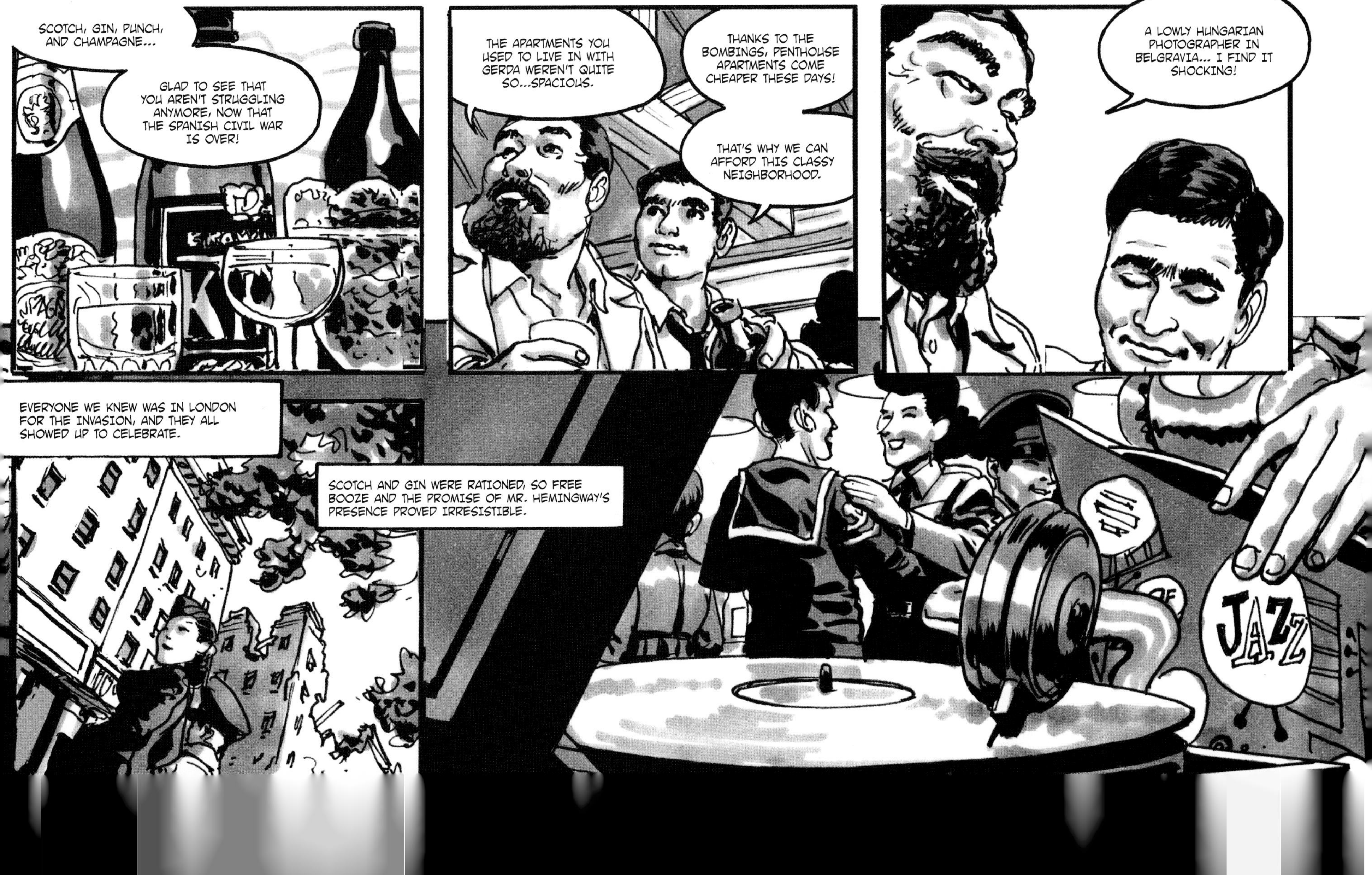
SCOTCH, GIN, PUNCH, AND CHAMPAGNE...
GLAD TO SEE THAT YOU AREN'T STRUGGLING ANYMORE, NOW THAT THE SPANISH CIVIL WAR IS OVER!
THE APARTMENTS YOU USED TO LIVE IN WITH GERDA WEREN'T QUITE SO...SPACIOUS.
THANKS TO THE BOMBINGS, PENTHOUSE APARTMENTS COME CHEAPER THESE DAYS!
THAT'S WHY WE CAN AFFORD THIS CLASSY NEIGHBORHOOD.
A LOWLY HUNGARIAN PHOTOGRAPHER IN BELGRAVIA... I FIND IT SHOCKING!
EVERYONE WE KNEW WAS IN LONDON FOR THE INVASION, AND THEY ALL SHOWED UP TO CELEBRATE.
SCOTCH AND GIN WERE RATIONED, SO FREE BOOZE AND THE PROMISE OF MR. HEMINGWAY'S PRESENCE PROVED IRRESISTIBLE.
JAZZ

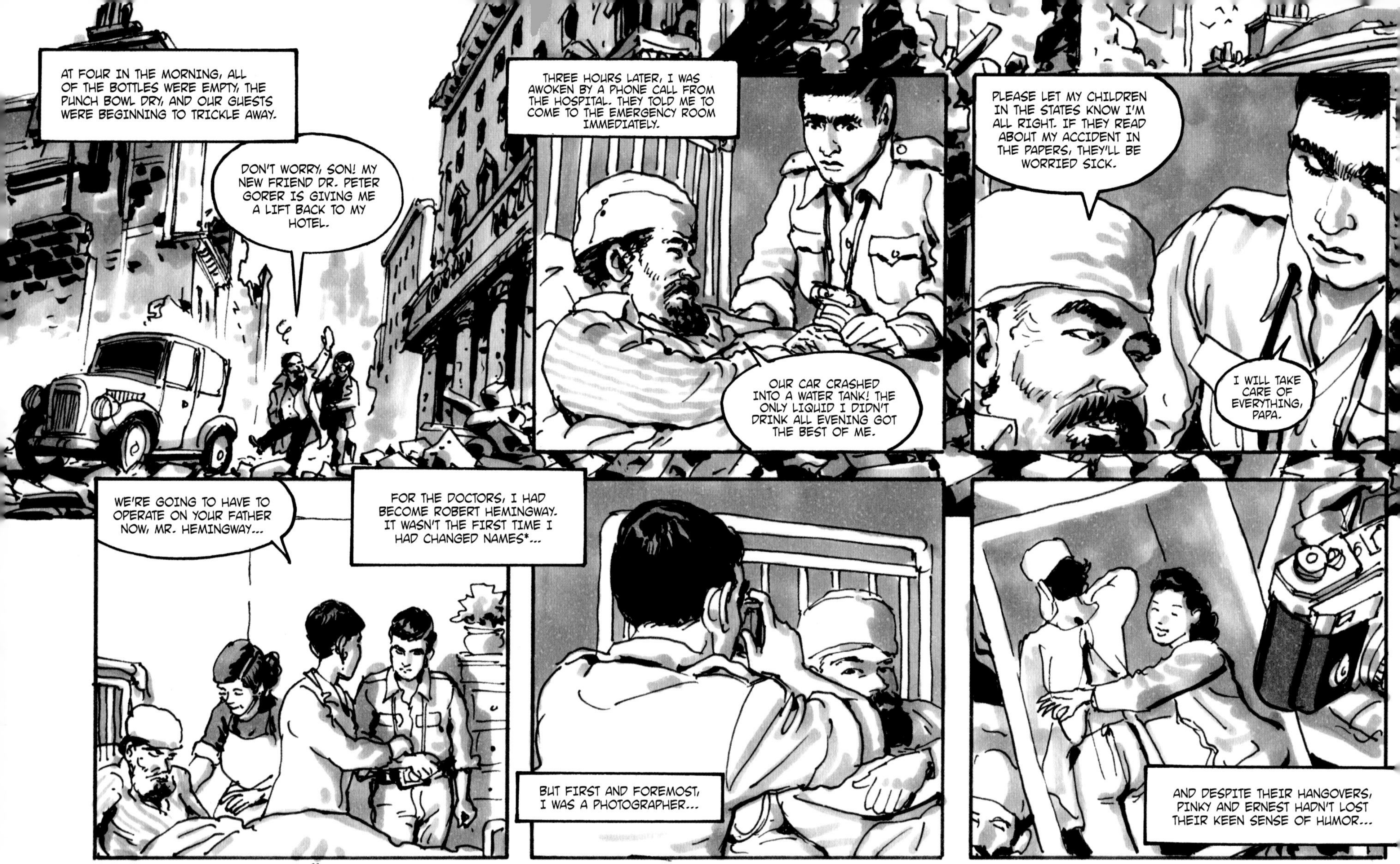
AT FOUR IN THE MORNING, ALL OF THE BOTTLES WERE EMPTY, THE PUNCH BOWL DRY, AND OUR GUESTS WERE BEGINNING TO TRICKLE AWAY.
DON'T WORRY, SON! MY NEW FRIEND DR. PETER GORER IS GIVING ME A LIFT BACK TO MY HOTEL.
THREE HOURS LATER, I WAS AWOKEN BY A PHONE CALL FROM THE HOSPITAL. THEY TOLD ME TO COME TO THE EMERGENCY ROOM IMMEDIATELY.
OUR CAR CRASHED INTO A WATER TANK! THE ONLY LIQUID I DIDN'T DRINK ALL EVENING GOT THE BEST OF ME.
PLEASE LET MY CHILDREN IN THE STATES KNOW I'M ALL RIGHT. IF THEY READ ABOUT MY ACCIDENT IN THE PAPERS, THEY'LL BE WORRIED SICK.
I WILL TAKE CARE OF EVERYTHING, PAPA.
WE'RE GOING TO HAVE TO OPERATE ON YOUR FATHER NOW, MR. HEMINGWAY...
FOR THE DOCTORS, I HAD BECOME ROBERT HEMINGWAY. IT WASN'T THE FIRST TIME I HAD CHANGED NAMES*...
BUT FIRST AND FOREMOST, I WAS A PHOTOGRAPHER...
AND DESPITE THEIR HANGOVERS, PINKY AND ERNEST HADN'T LOST THEIR KEEN SENSE OF HUMOR...

*CAPA'S REAL NAME WAS ENDRE ERNÖ FRIEDMANN.

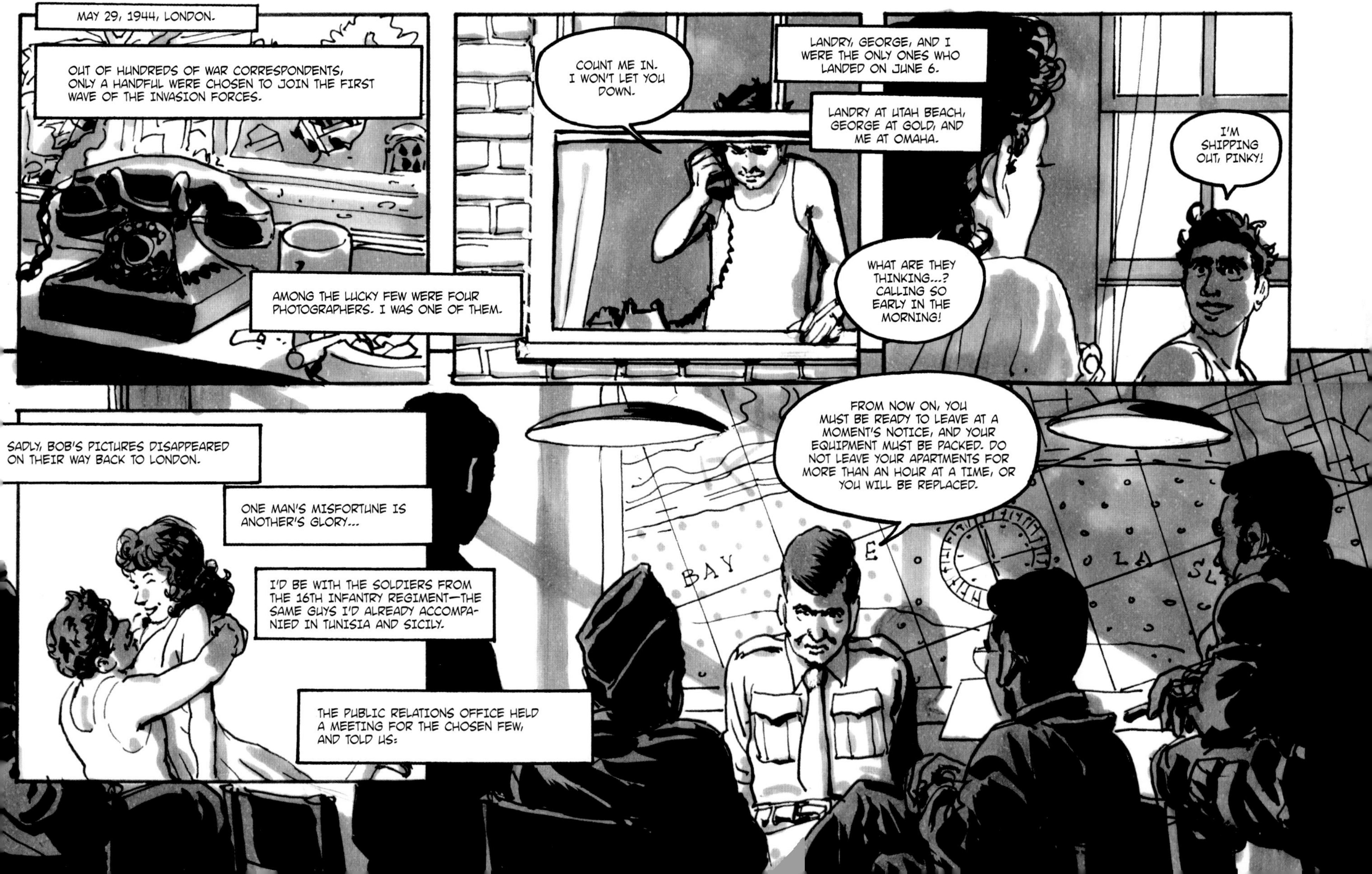
MAY 29, 1944, LONDON.
OUT OF HUNDREDS OF WAR CORRESPONDENTS, ONLY A HANDFUL WERE CHOSEN TO JOIN THE FIRST WAVE OF THE INVASION FORCES.
AMONG THE LUCKY FEW WERE FOUR PHOTOGRAPHERS. I WAS ONE OF THEM.
COUNT ME IN. I WON'T LET YOU DOWN.
LANDRY, GEORGE, AND I WERE THE ONLY ONES WHO LANDED ON JUNE 6.
LANDRY AT UTAH BEACH, GEORGE AT GOLD, AND ME AT OMAHA.
WHAT ARE THEY THINKING...? CALLING SO EARLY IN THE MORNING!
I'M SHIPPING OUT, PINKY!
SADLY, BOB'S PICTURES DISAPPEARED ON THEIR WAY BACK TO LONDON.
ONE MAN'S MISFORTUNE IS ANOTHER'S GLORY...
I'D BE WITH THE SOLDIERS FROM THE 16TH INFANTRY REGIMENT—THE SAME GUYS I'D ALREADY ACCOMPANIED IN TUNISIA AND SICILY.
THE PUBLIC RELATIONS OFFICE HELD A MEETING FOR THE CHOSEN FEW, AND TOLD US:
FROM NOW ON, YOU MUST BE READY TO LEAVE AT A MOMENT'S NOTICE, AND YOUR EQUIPMENT MUST BE PACKED. DO NOT LEAVE YOUR APARTMENTS FOR MORE THAN AN HOUR AT A TIME, OR YOU WILL BE REPLACED.
BAY

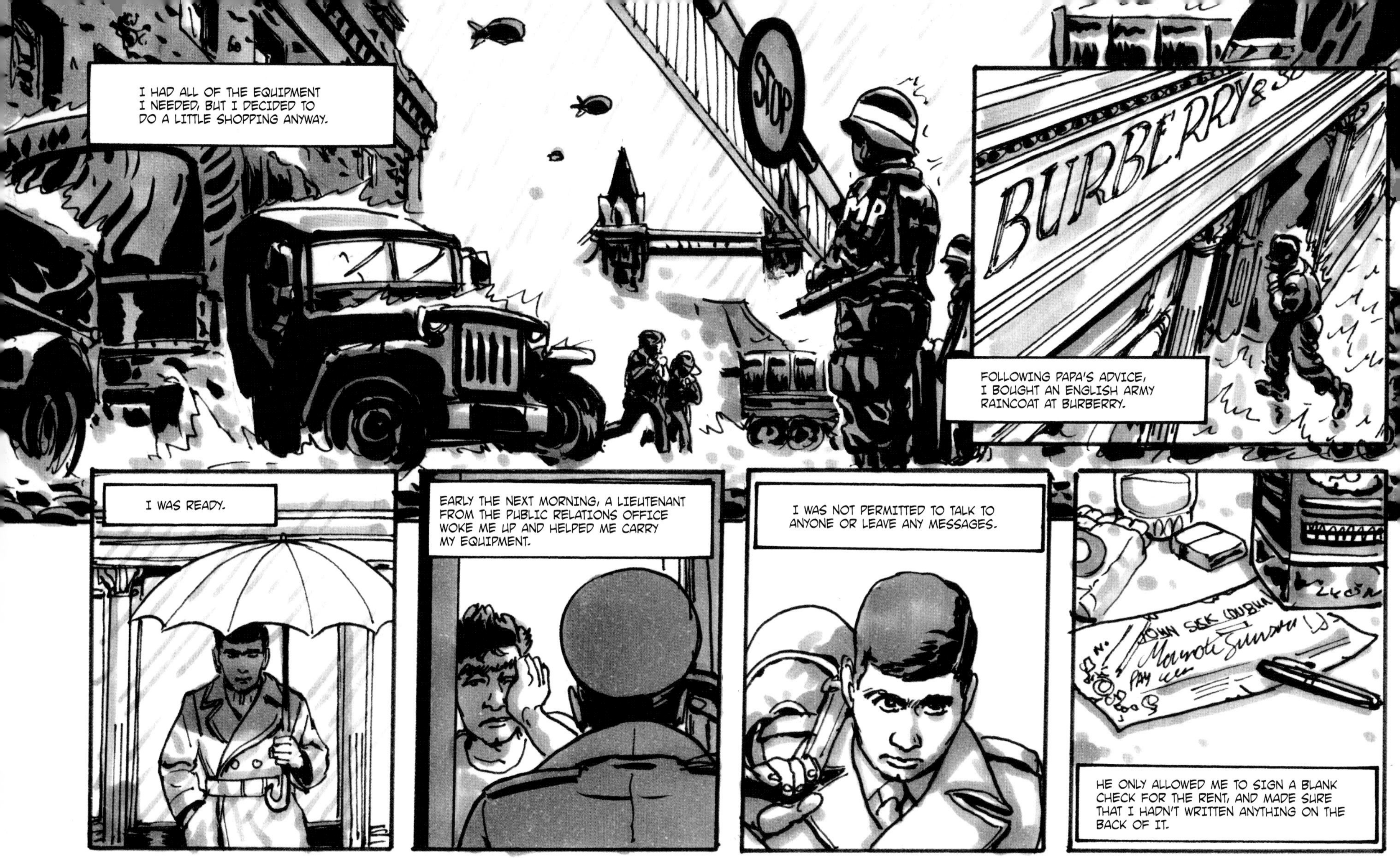
I HAD ALL OF THE EQUIPMENT I NEEDED, BUT I DECIDED TO DO A LITTLE SHOPPING ANYWAY.
STOP
MP
BURBERRY
FOLLOWING PAPA'S ADVICE, I BOUGHT AN ENGLISH ARMY RAINCOAT AT BURBERRY.
I WAS READY.
EARLY THE NEXT MORNING, A LIEUTENANT FROM THE PUBLIC RELATIONS OFFICE WOKE ME UP AND HELPED ME CARRY MY EQUIPMENT.
I WAS NOT PERMITTED TO TALK TO ANYONE OR LEAVE ANY MESSAGES.
HE ONLY ALLOWED ME TO SIGN A BLANK CHECK FOR THE RENT, AND MADE SURE THAT I HADN'T WRITTEN ANYTHING ON THE BACK OF IT.

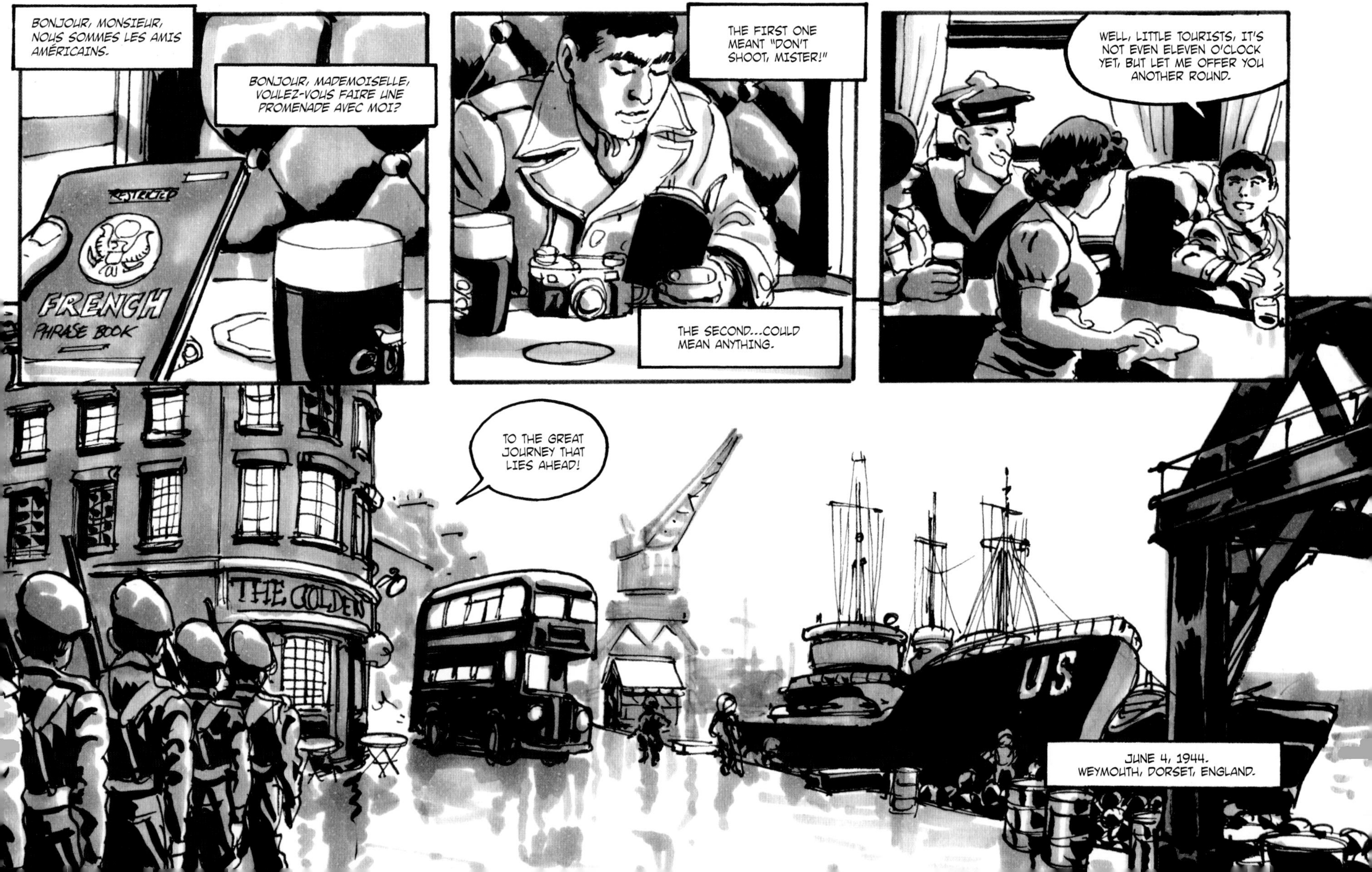
BONJOUR, MONSIEUR, NOUS SOMMES LES AMIS AMÉRICAINS.
BONJOUR, MADEMOISELLE, VOULEZ-VOUS FAIRE UNE PROMENADE AVEC MOI?
FRENCH PHRASE BOOK
THE FIRST ONE MEANT "DON'T SHOOT, MISTER!"
THE SECOND...COULD MEAN ANYTHING.
WELL, LITTLE TOURISTS, IT'S NOT EVEN ELEVEN O'CLOCK YET, BUT LET ME OFFER YOU ANOTHER ROUND.
TO THE GREAT JOURNEY THAT LIES AHEAD!
THE GOLDEN
US
JUNE 4, 1944.
WEYMOUTH, DORSET, ENGLAND.

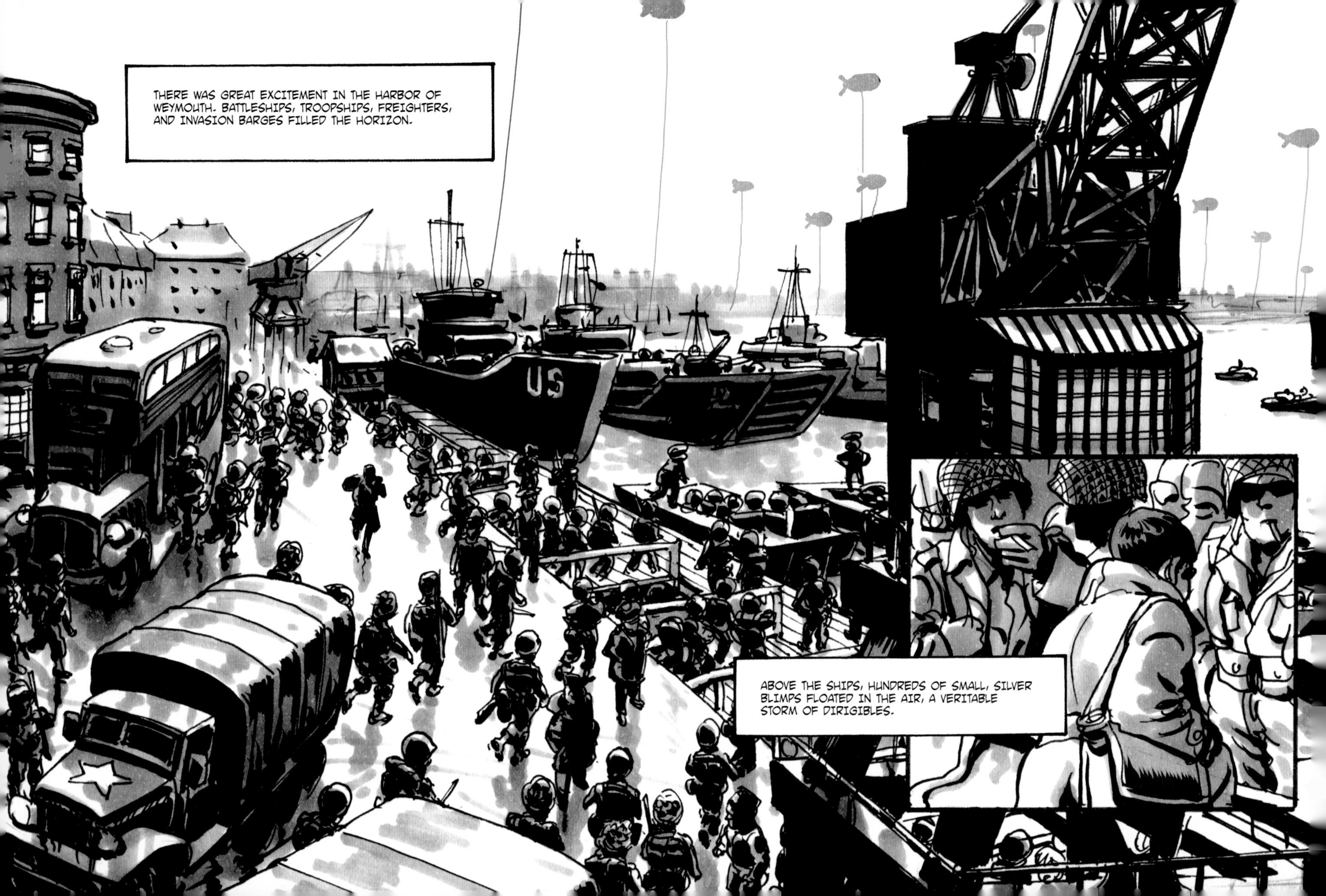
THERE WAS GREAT EXCITEMENT IN THE HARBOR OF WEYMOUTH. BATTLESHIPS, TROOPSHIPS, FREIGHTERS, AND INVASION BARGES FILLED THE HORIZON.
US
ABOVE THE SHIPS, HUNDREDS OF SMALL, SILVER BLIMPS FLOATED IN THE AIR, A VERITABLE STORM OF DIRIGIBLES.

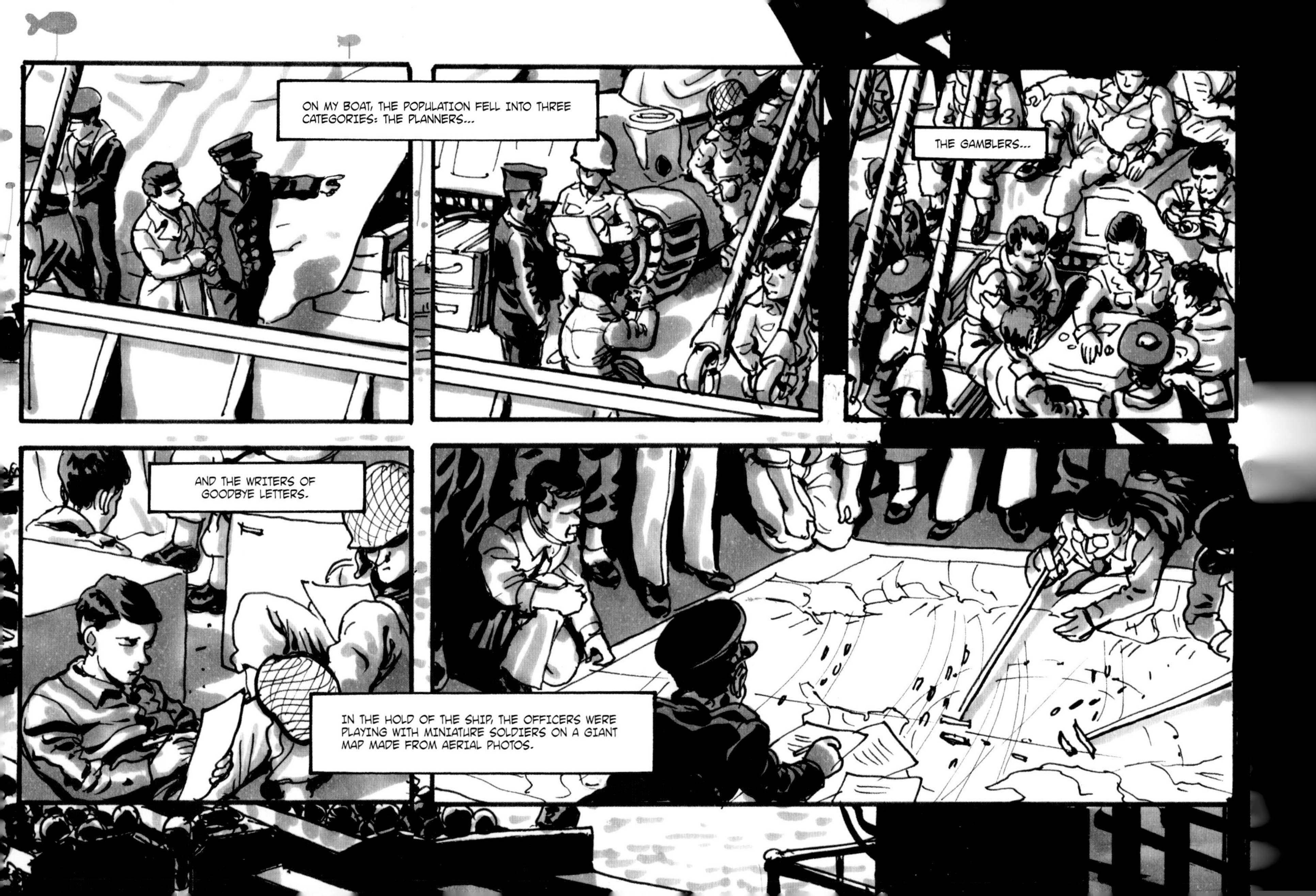
ON MY BOAT, THE POPULATION FELL INTO THREE CATEGORIES: THE PLANNERS...
THE GAMBLERS...
AND THE WRITERS OF GOODBYE LETTERS.
IN THE HOLD OF THE SHIP, THE OFFICERS WERE PLAYING WITH MINIATURE SOLDIERS ON A GIANT MAP MADE FROM AERIAL PHOTOS.

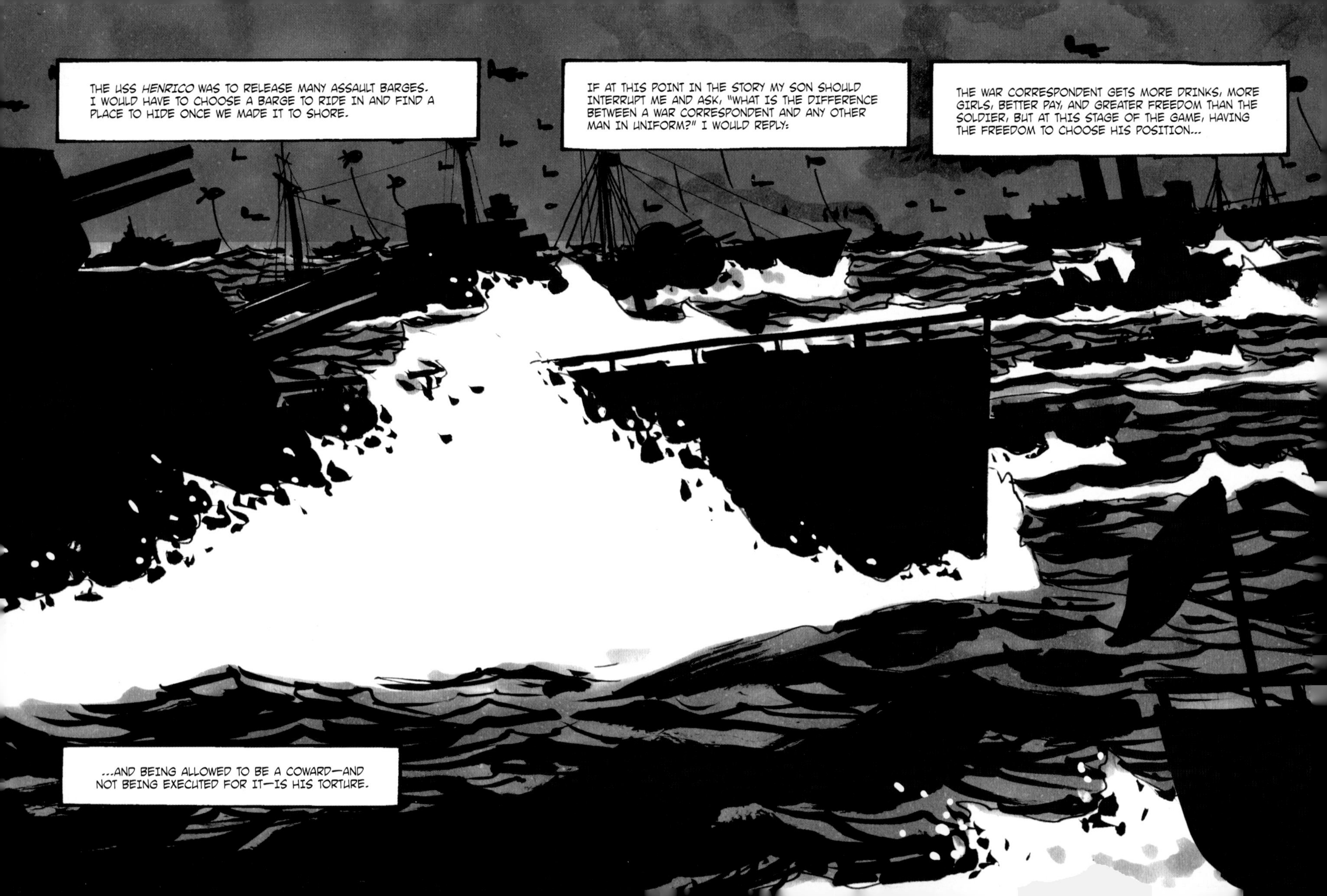
THE USS *HENRICO* WAS TO RELEASE MANY ASSAULT BARGES. I WOULD HAVE TO CHOOSE A BARGE TO RIDE IN AND FIND A PLACE TO HIDE ONCE WE MADE IT TO SHORE.
IF AT THIS POINT IN THE STORY MY SON SHOULD INTERRUPT ME AND ASK, "WHAT IS THE DIFFERENCE BETWEEN A WAR CORRESPONDENT AND ANY OTHER MAN IN UNIFORM?" I WOULD REPLY:
THE WAR CORRESPONDENT GETS MORE DRINKS, MORE GIRLS, BETTER PAY, AND GREATER FREEDOM THAN THE SOLDIER, BUT AT THIS STAGE OF THE GAME, HAVING THE FREEDOM TO CHOOSE HIS POSITION...
...AND BEING ALLOWED TO BE A COWARD—AND NOT BEING EXECUTED FOR IT—IS HIS TORTURE.

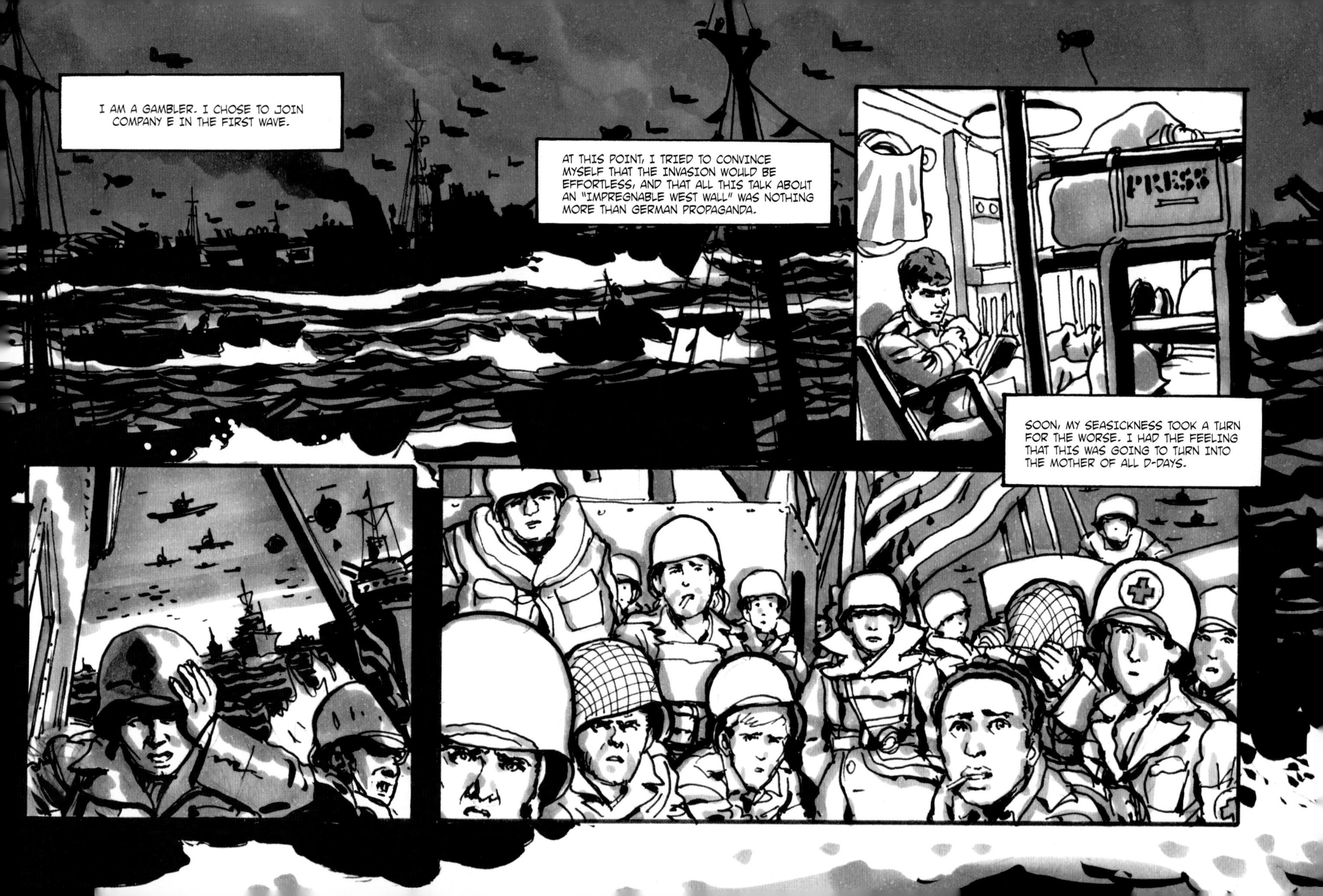
I AM A GAMBLER. I CHOSE TO JOIN COMPANY E IN THE FIRST WAVE.
AT THIS POINT, I TRIED TO CONVINCE MYSELF THAT THE INVASION WOULD BE EFFORTLESS, AND THAT ALL THIS TALK ABOUT AN "IMPREGNABLE WEST WALL" WAS NOTHING MORE THAN GERMAN PROPAGANDA.
PRESS
SOON, MY SEASICKNESS TOOK A TURN FOR THE WORSE. I HAD THE FEELING THAT THIS WAS GOING TO TURN INTO THE MOTHER OF ALL D-DAYS.

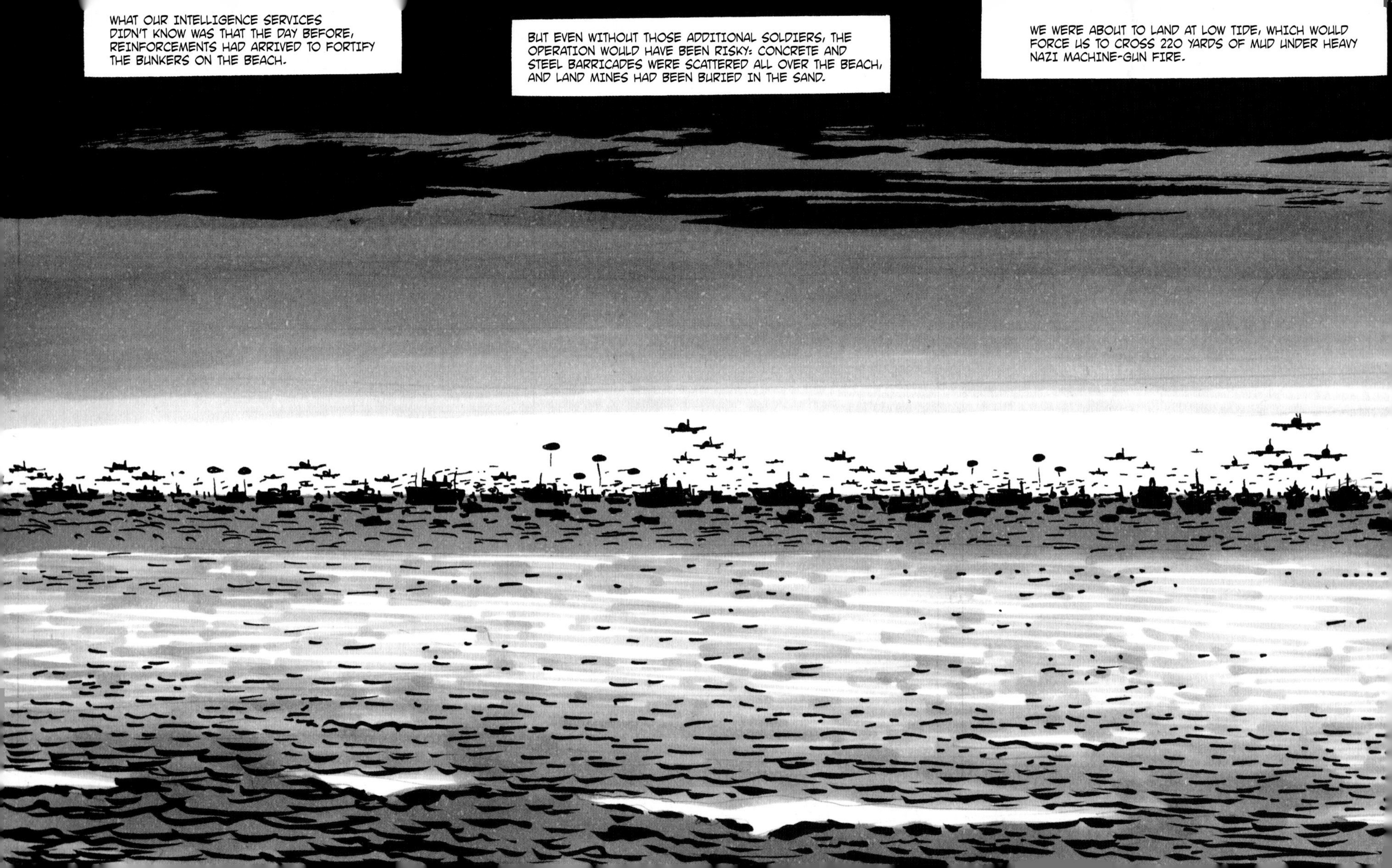
WHAT OUR INTELLIGENCE SERVICES DIDN'T KNOW WAS THAT THE DAY BEFORE, REINFORCEMENTS HAD ARRIVED TO FORTIFY THE BUNKERS ON THE BEACH.
BUT EVEN WITHOUT THOSE ADDITIONAL SOLDIERS, THE OPERATION WOULD HAVE BEEN RISKY: CONCRETE AND STEEL BARRICADES WERE SCATTERED ALL OVER THE BEACH, AND LAND MINES HAD BEEN BURIED IN THE SAND.
WE WERE ABOUT TO LAND AT LOW TIDE, WHICH WOULD FORCE US TO CROSS 220 YARDS OF MUD UNDER HEAVY NAZI MACHINE-GUN FIRE.

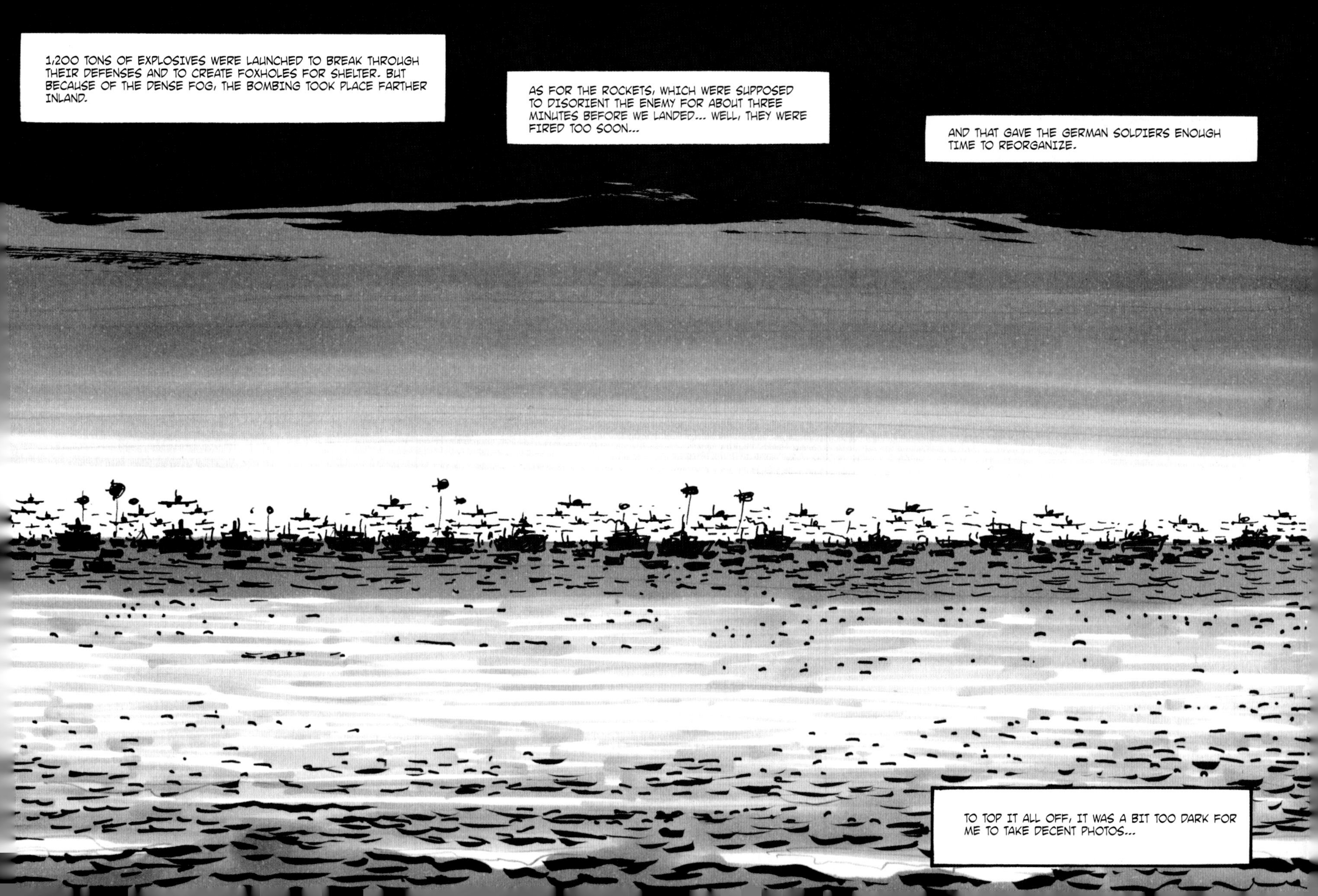
1,200 TONS OF EXPLOSIVES WERE LAUNCHED TO BREAK THROUGH THEIR DEFENSES AND TO CREATE FOXHOLES FOR SHELTER. BUT BECAUSE OF THE DENSE FOG, THE BOMBING TOOK PLACE FARTHER INLAND.
AS FOR THE ROCKETS, WHICH WERE SUPPOSED TO DISORIENT THE ENEMY FOR ABOUT THREE MINUTES BEFORE WE LANDED... WELL, THEY WERE FIRED TOO SOON...
AND THAT GAVE THE GERMAN SOLDIERS ENOUGH TIME TO REORGANIZE.
TO TOP IT ALL OFF, IT WAS A BIT TOO DARK FOR ME TO TAKE DECENT PHOTOS...

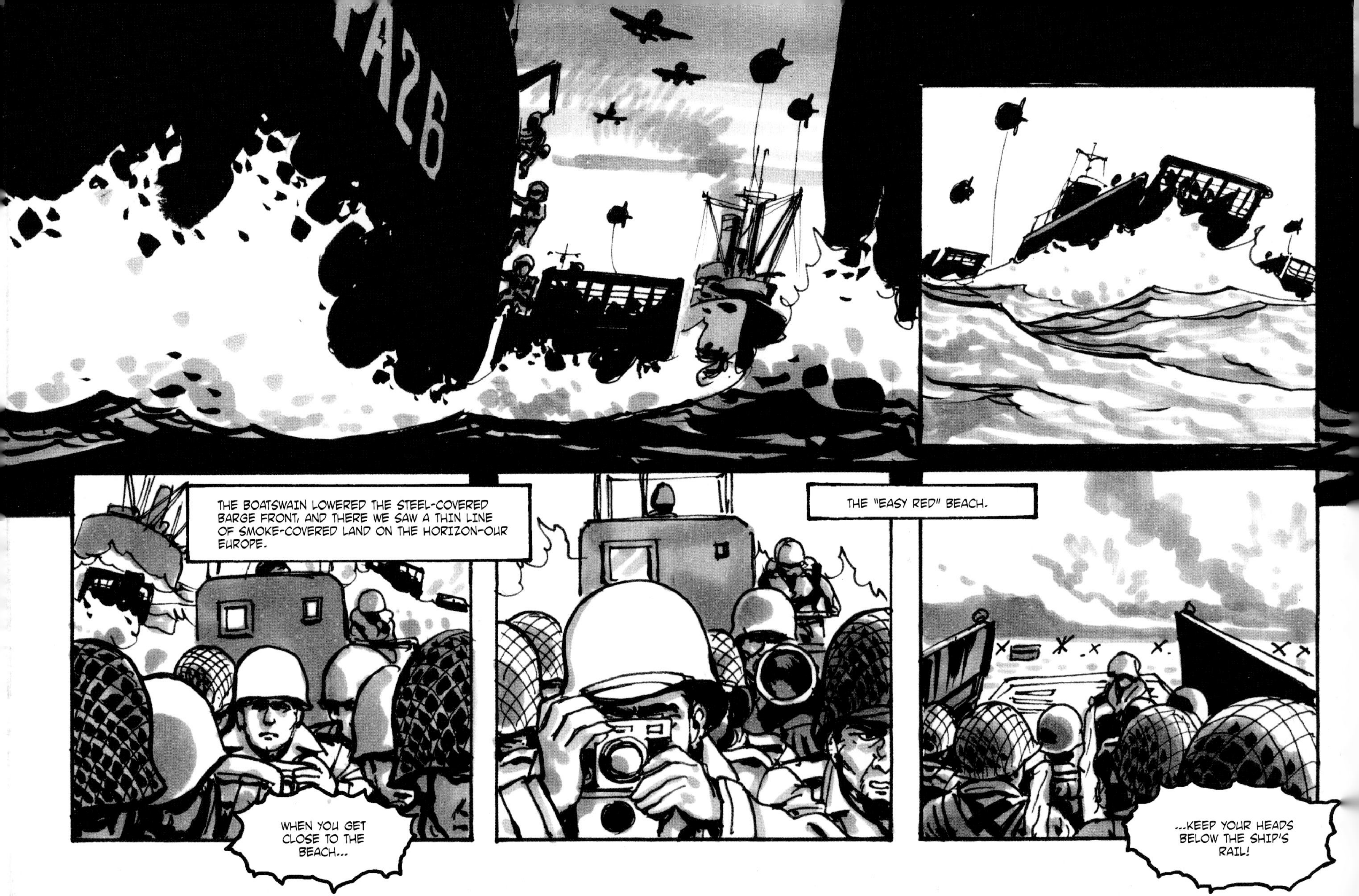

THE BOATSWAIN LOWERED THE STEEL-COVERED BARGE FRONT, AND THERE WE SAW A THIN LINE OF SMOKE-COVERED LAND ON THE HORIZON—OUR EUROPE.
WHEN YOU GET CLOSE TO THE BEACH...
THE "EASY RED" BEACH.
...KEEP YOUR HEADS BELOW THE SHIP'S RAIL!

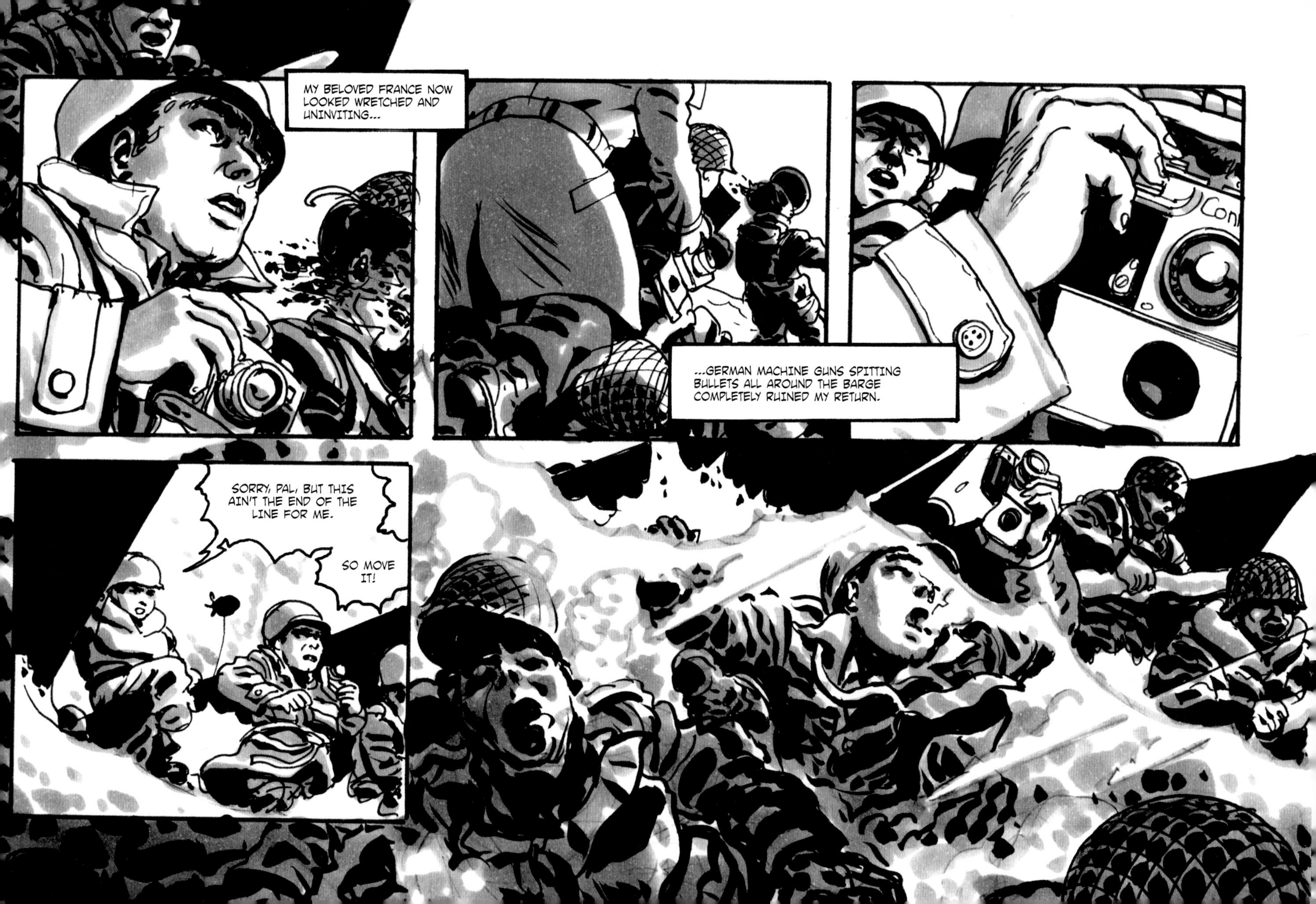
MY BELOVED FRANCE NOW LOOKED WRETCHED AND UNINVITING...
...GERMAN MACHINE GUNS SPITTING BULLETS ALL AROUND THE BARGE COMPLETELY RUINED MY RETURN.
SORRY, PAL, BUT THIS AIN'T THE END OF THE LINE FOR ME.
SO MOVE IT!

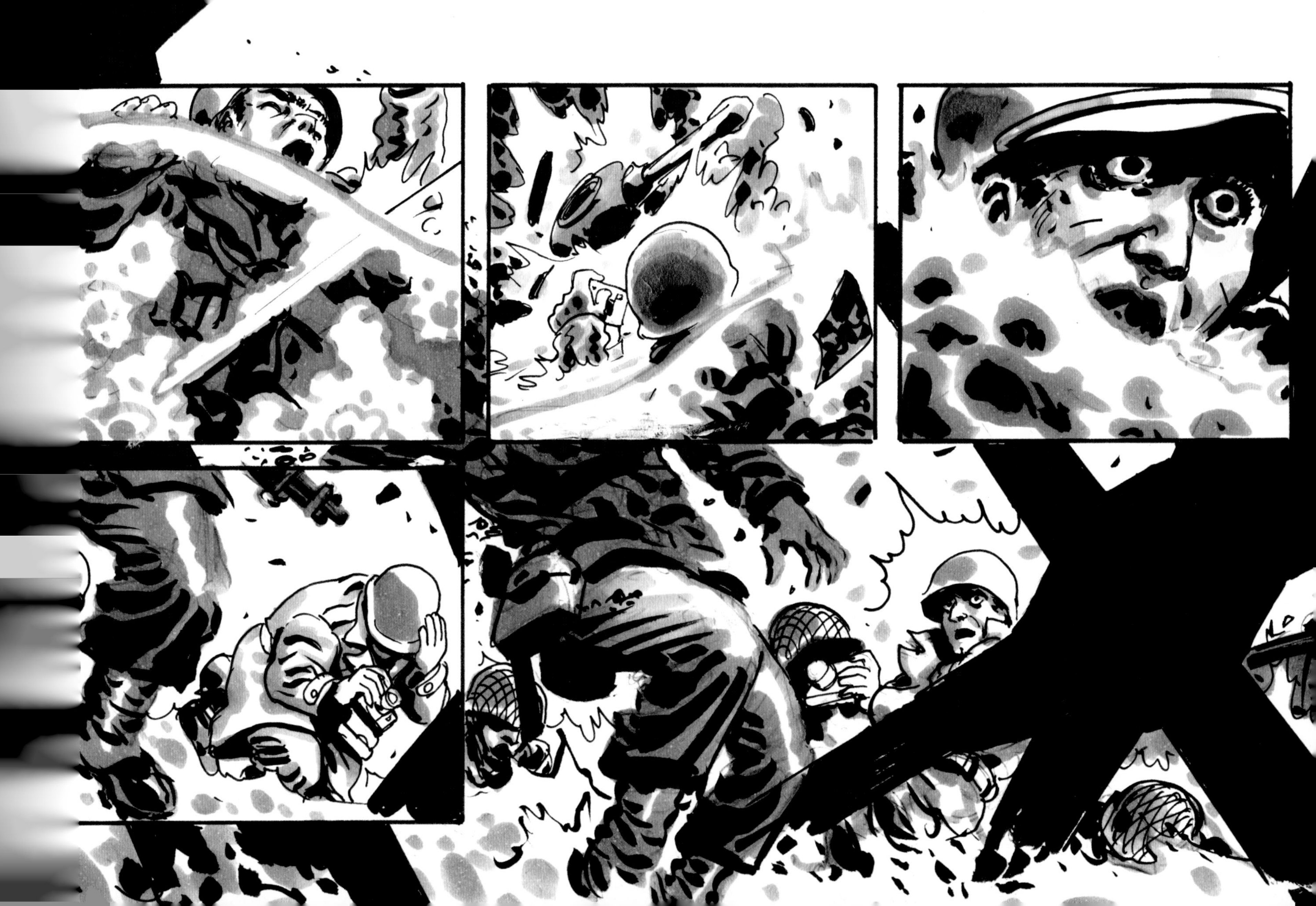

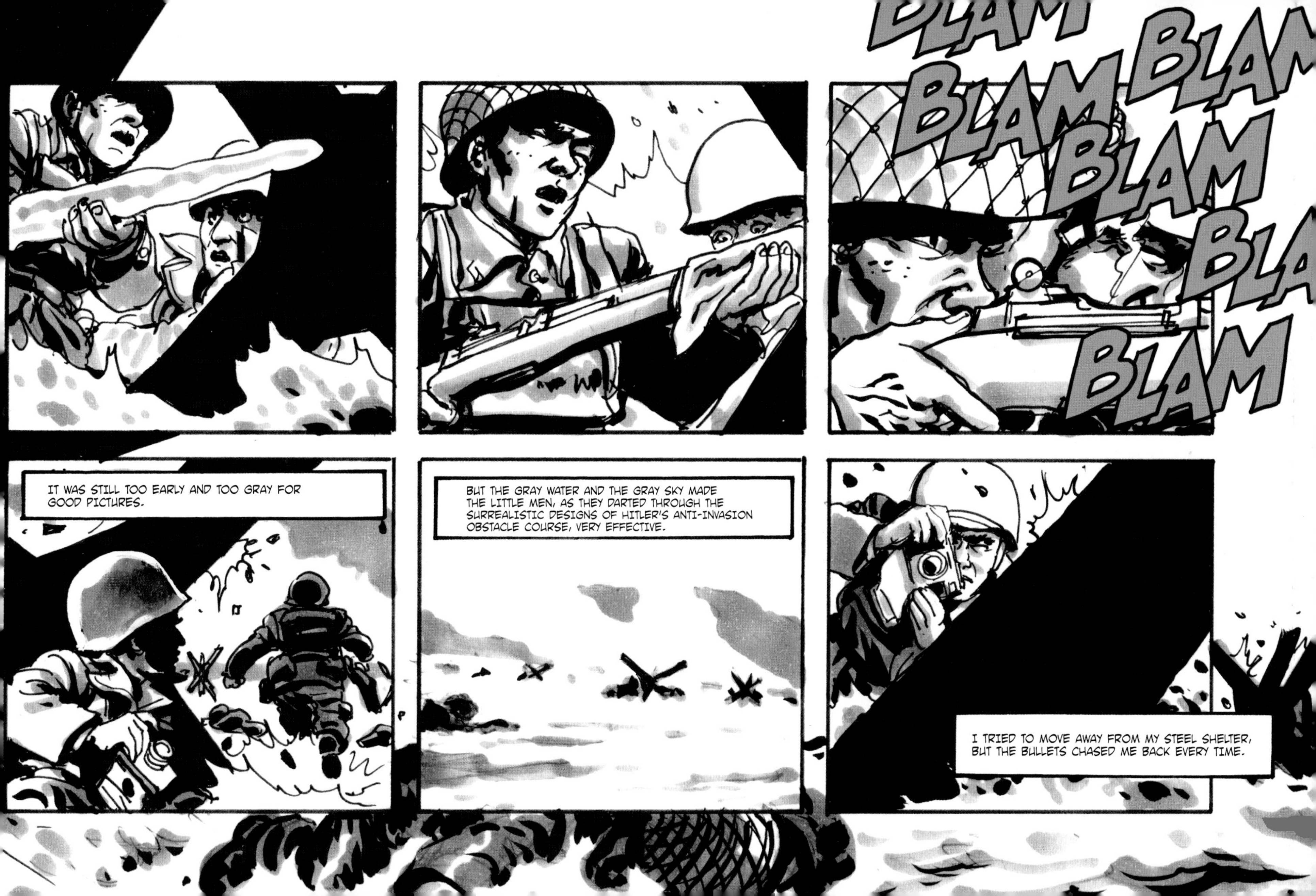
BLAM
BLAM BLAM
BLAM
BLAM
BLA
BLAM
IT WAS STILL TOO EARLY AND TOO GRAY FOR GOOD PICTURES.
BUT THE GRAY WATER AND THE GRAY SKY MADE THE LITTLE MEN, AS THEY DARTED THROUGH THE SURREALISTIC DESIGNS OF HITLER'S ANTI-INVASION OBSTACLE COURSE, VERY EFFECTIVE.
I TRIED TO MOVE AWAY FROM MY STEEL SHELTER, BUT THE BULLETS CHASED ME BACK EVERY TIME.

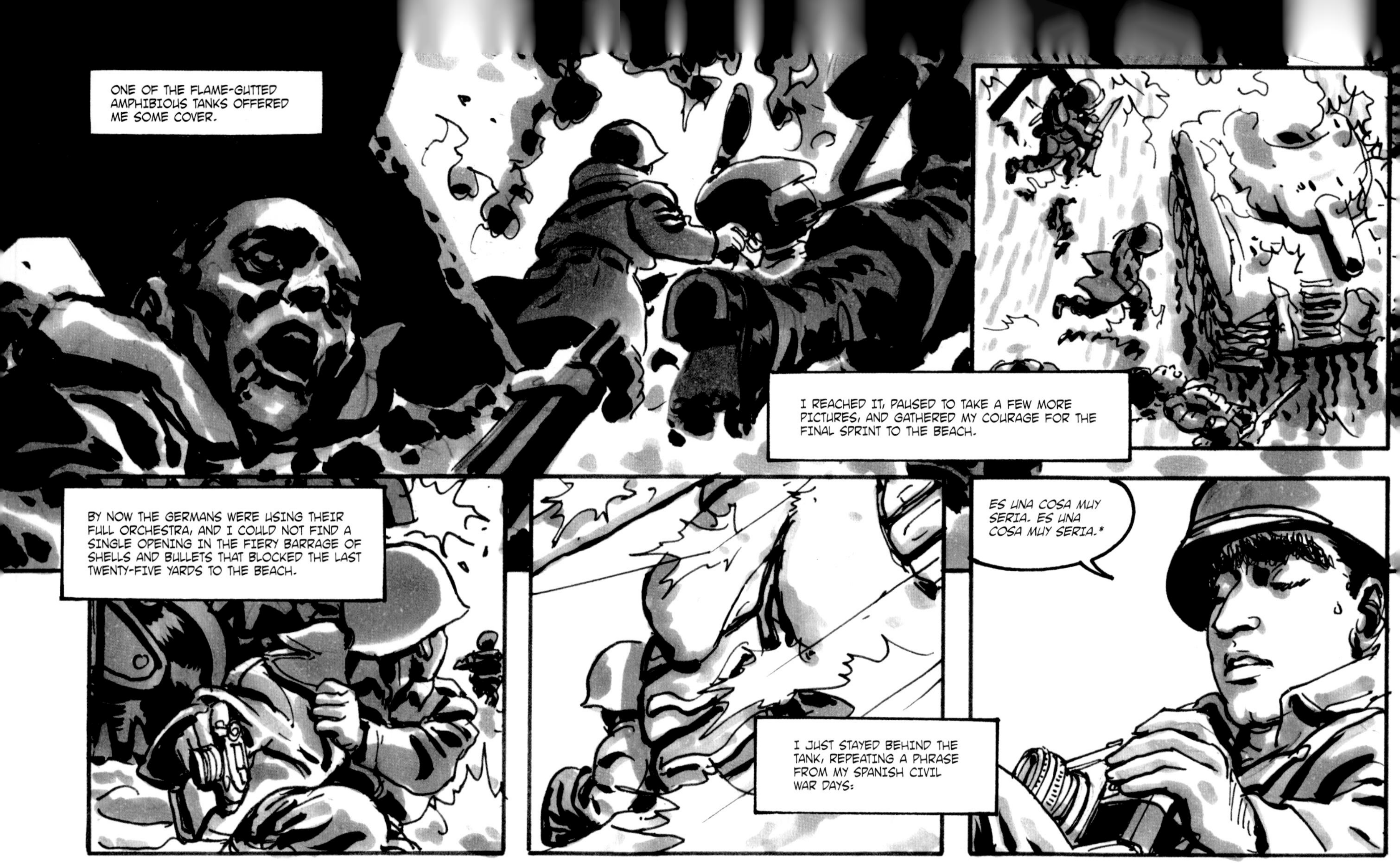
ONE OF THE FLAME-GUTTED AMPHIBIOUS TANKS OFFERED ME SOME COVER.
I REACHED IT, PAUSED TO TAKE A FEW MORE PICTURES, AND GATHERED MY COURAGE FOR THE FINAL SPRINT TO THE BEACH.
BY NOW THE GERMANS WERE USING THEIR FULL ORCHESTRA, AND I COULD NOT FIND A SINGLE OPENING IN THE FIERY BARRAGE OF SHELLS AND BULLETS THAT BLOCKED THE LAST TWENTY-FIVE YARDS TO THE BEACH.
I JUST STAYED BEHIND THE TANK, REPEATING A PHRASE FROM MY SPANISH CIVIL WAR DAYS:
ES UNA COSA MUY SERIA. ES UNA COSA MUY SERIA.*

*"THIS IS VERY SERIOUS BUSINESS."

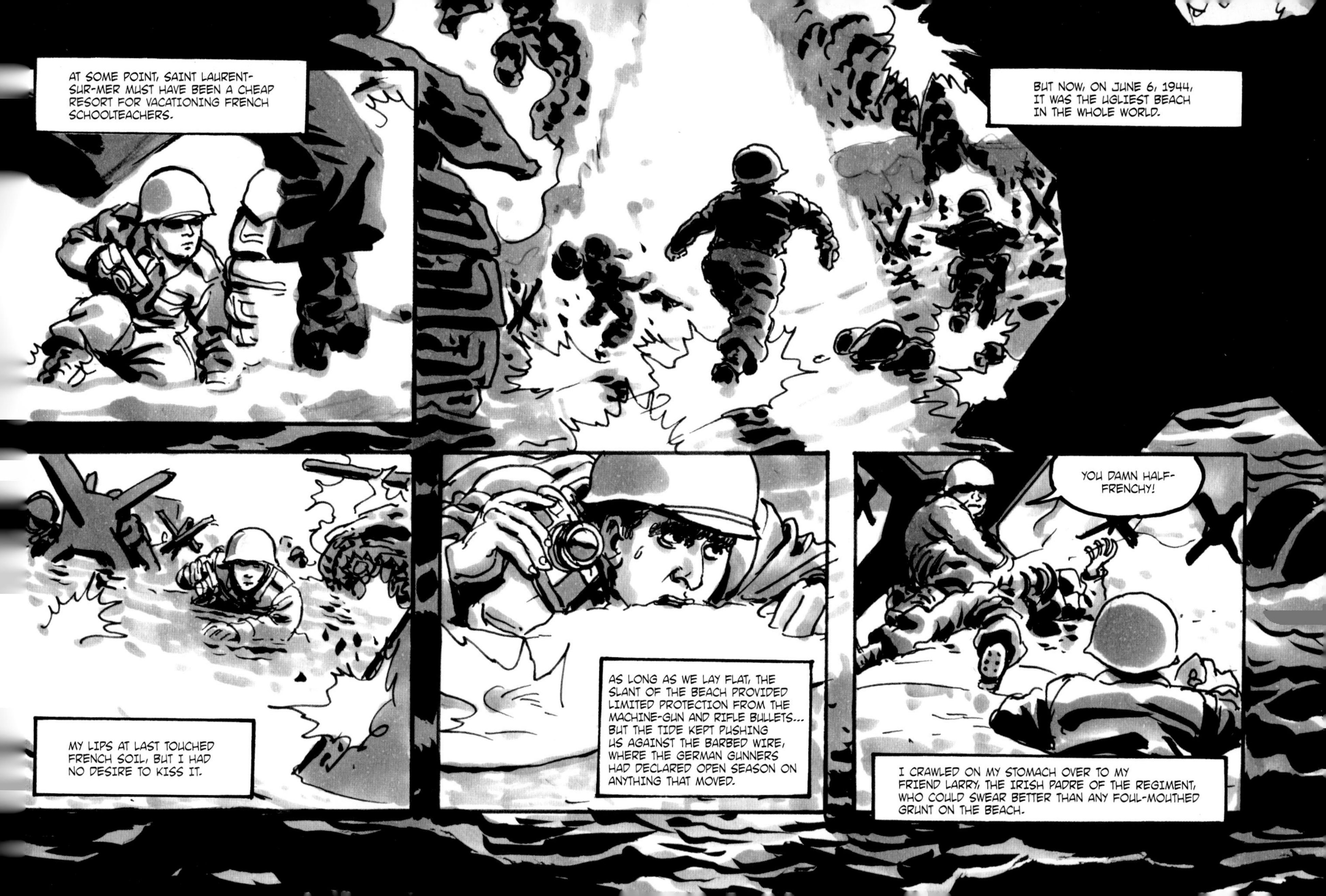
AT SOME POINT, SAINT LAURENT-SUR-MER MUST HAVE BEEN A CHEAP RESORT FOR VACATIONING FRENCH SCHOOLTEACHERS.
BUT NOW, ON JUNE 6, 1944, IT WAS THE UGLIEST BEACH IN THE WHOLE WORLD.
MY LIPS AT LAST TOUCHED FRENCH SOIL, BUT I HAD NO DESIRE TO KISS IT.
AS LONG AS WE LAY FLAT, THE SLANT OF THE BEACH PROVIDED LIMITED PROTECTION FROM THE MACHINE-GUN AND RIFLE BULLETS... BUT THE TIDE KEPT PUSHING US AGAINST THE BARBED WIRE, WHERE THE GERMAN GUNNERS HAD DECLARED OPEN SEASON ON ANYTHING THAT MOVED.
YOU DAMN HALF-FRENCHY!
I CRAWLED ON MY STOMACH OVER TO MY FRIEND LARRY, THE IRISH PADRE OF THE REGIMENT, WHO COULD SWEAR BETTER THAN ANY FOUL-MOUTHED GRUNT ON THE BEACH.

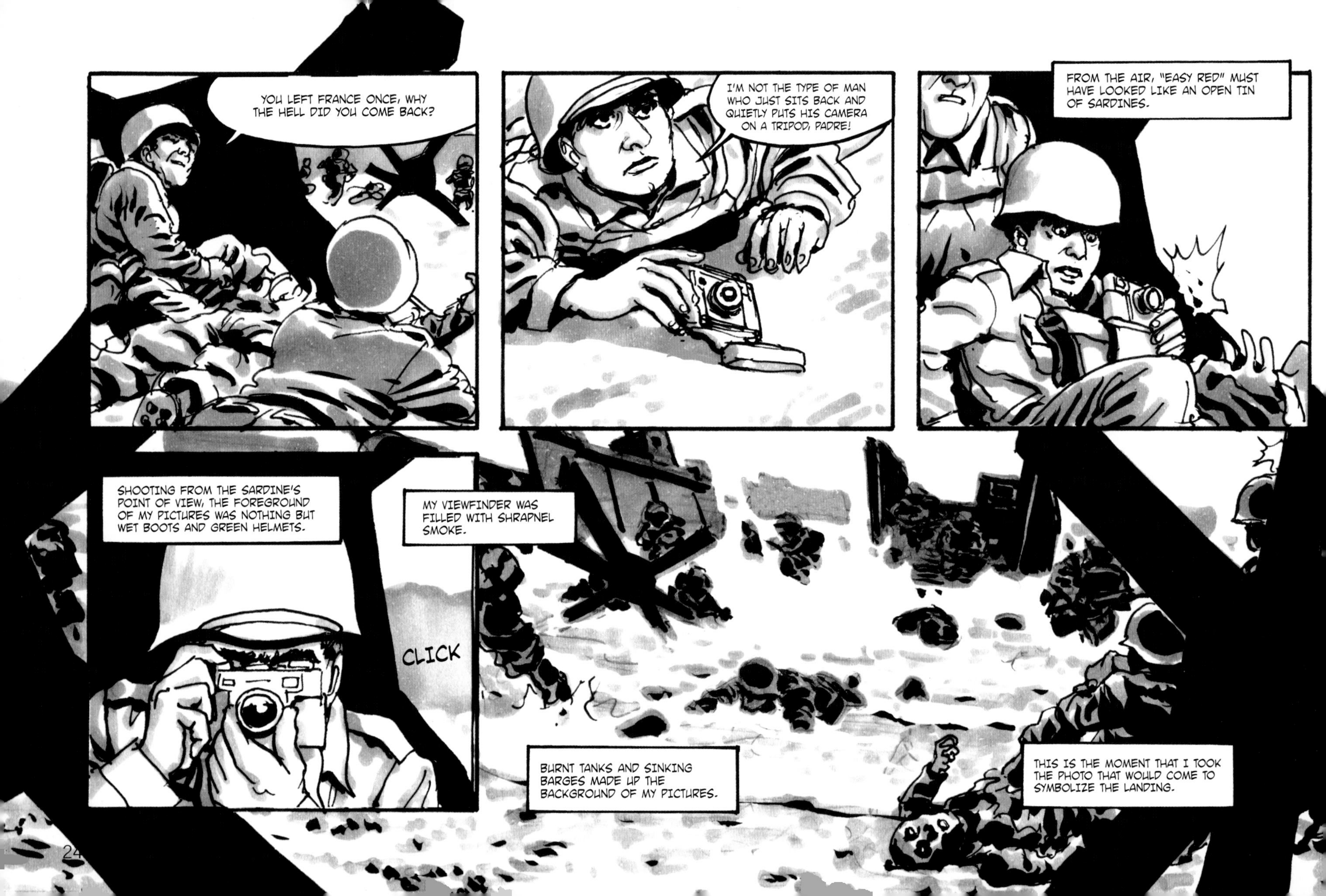

YOU LEFT FRANCE ONCE, WHY THE HELL DID YOU COME BACK?
I'M NOT THE TYPE OF MAN WHO JUST SITS BACK AND QUIETLY PUTS HIS CAMERA ON A TRIPOD, PADRE!
FROM THE AIR, "EASY RED" MUST HAVE LOOKED LIKE AN OPEN TIN OF SARDINES.
SHOOTING FROM THE SARDINE'S POINT OF VIEW, THE FOREGROUND OF MY PICTURES WAS NOTHING BUT WET BOOTS AND GREEN HELMETS.
MY VIEWFINDER WAS FILLED WITH SHRAPNEL SMOKE.
CLICK
BURNT TANKS AND SINKING BARGES MADE UP THE BACKGROUND OF MY PICTURES.
THIS IS THE MOMENT THAT I TOOK THE PHOTO THAT WOULD COME TO SYMBOLIZE THE LANDING.

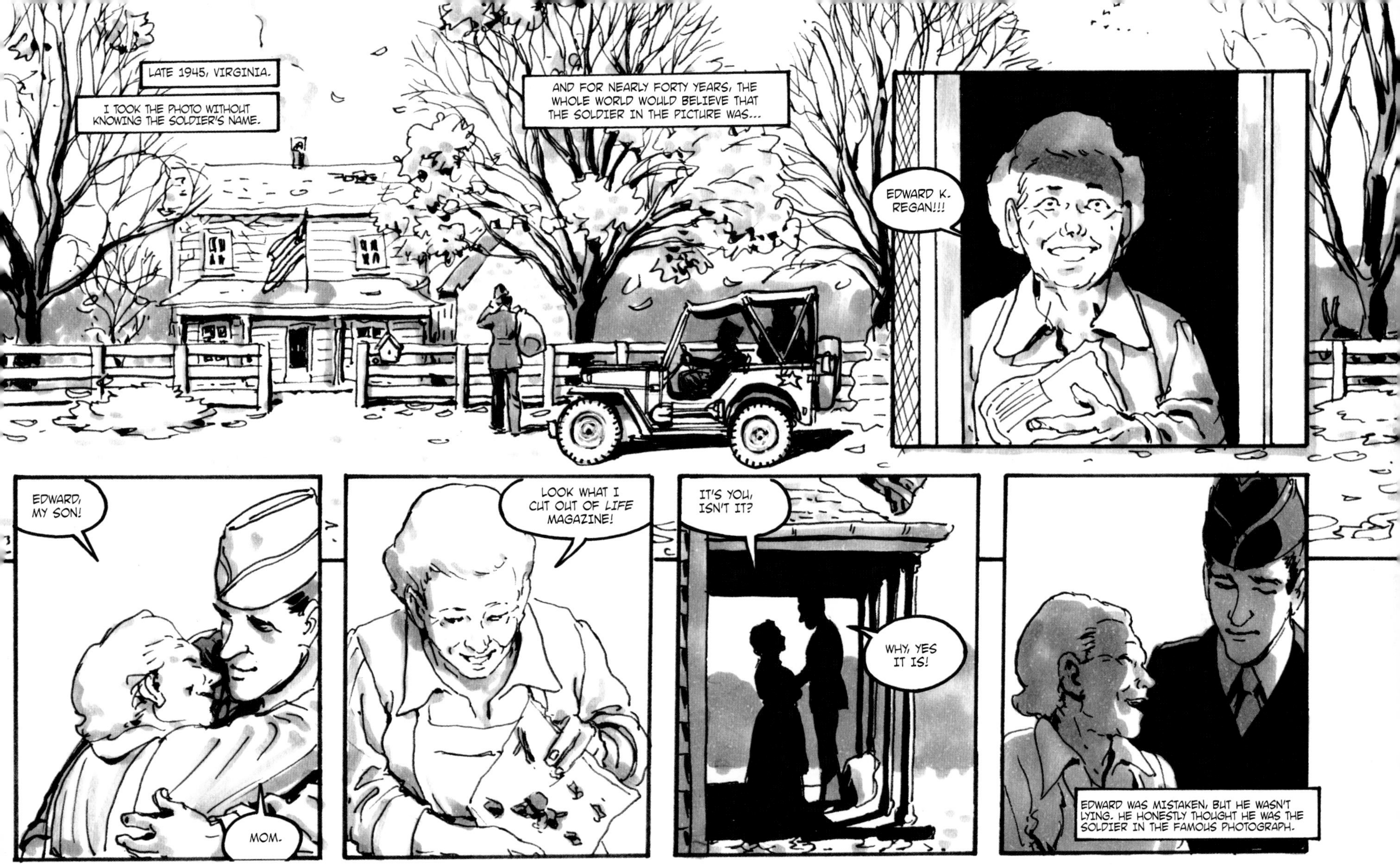
LATE 1945, VIRGINIA.
I TOOK THE PHOTO WITHOUT KNOWING THE SOLDIER'S NAME.
AND FOR NEARLY FORTY YEARS, THE WHOLE WORLD WOULD BELIEVE THAT THE SOLDIER IN THE PICTURE WAS...
EDWARD K. REGAN!!!
EDWARD, MY SON!
MOM.
LOOK WHAT I CUT OUT OF *LIFE* MAGAZINE!
IT'S YOU, ISN'T IT?
WHY, YES IT IS!
EDWARD WAS MISTAKEN, BUT HE WASN'T LYING. HE HONESTLY THOUGHT HE WAS THE SOLDIER IN THE FAMOUS PHOTOGRAPH.

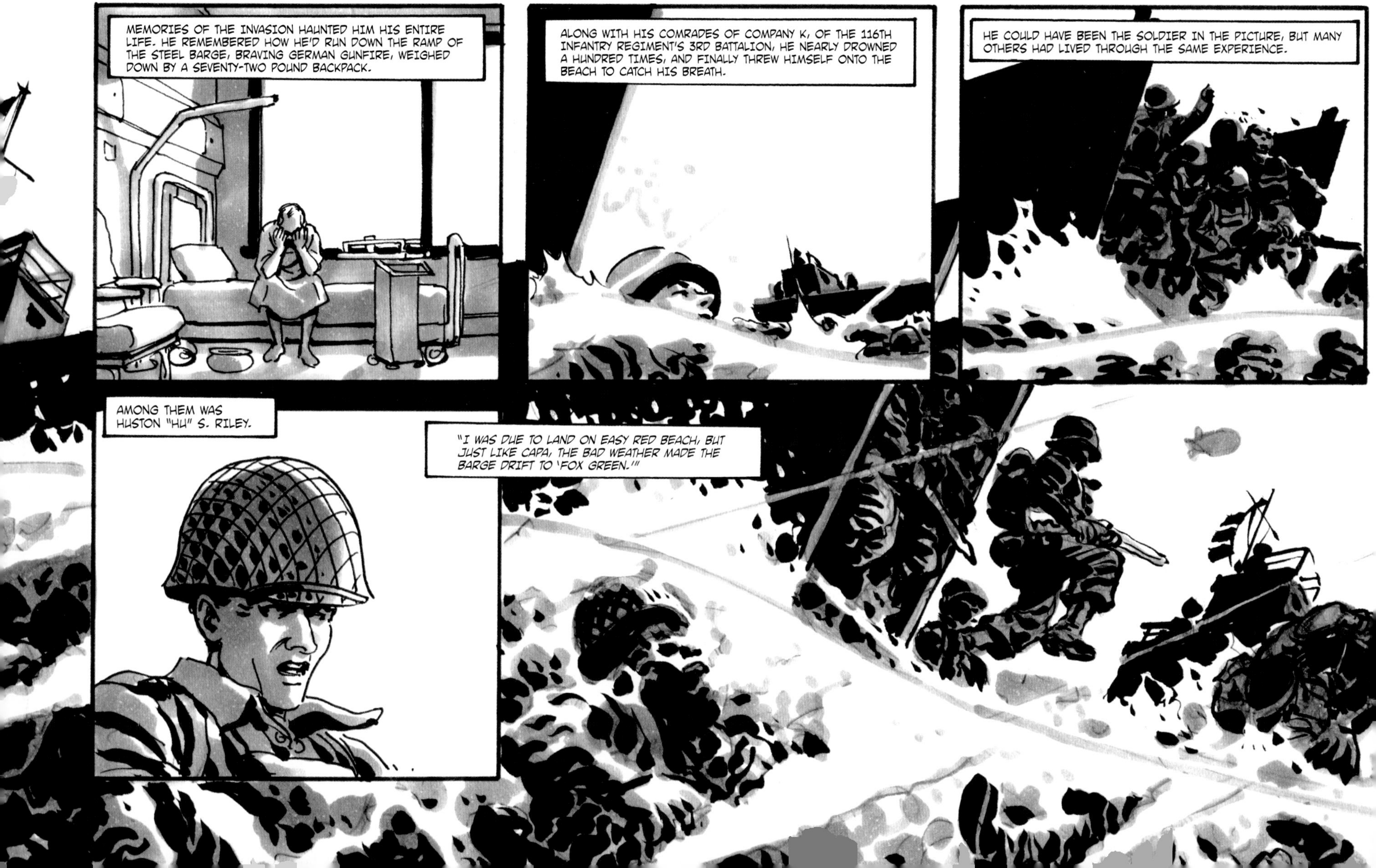
MEMORIES OF THE INVASION HAUNTED HIM HIS ENTIRE LIFE. HE REMEMBERED HOW HE'D RUN DOWN THE RAMP OF THE STEEL BARGE, BRAVING GERMAN GUNFIRE, WEIGHED DOWN BY A SEVENTY-TWO POUND BACKPACK.
ALONG WITH HIS COMRADES OF COMPANY K, OF THE 116TH INFANTRY REGIMENT'S 3RD BATTALION, HE NEARLY DROWNED A HUNDRED TIMES, AND FINALLY THREW HIMSELF ONTO THE BEACH TO CATCH HIS BREATH.
HE COULD HAVE BEEN THE SOLDIER IN THE PICTURE, BUT MANY OTHERS HAD LIVED THROUGH THE SAME EXPERIENCE.
AMONG THEM WAS HUSTON "HU" S. RILEY.
"I WAS DUE TO LAND ON EASY RED BEACH, BUT JUST LIKE CAPA, THE BAD WEATHER MADE THE BARGE DRIFT TO 'FOX GREEN.'"

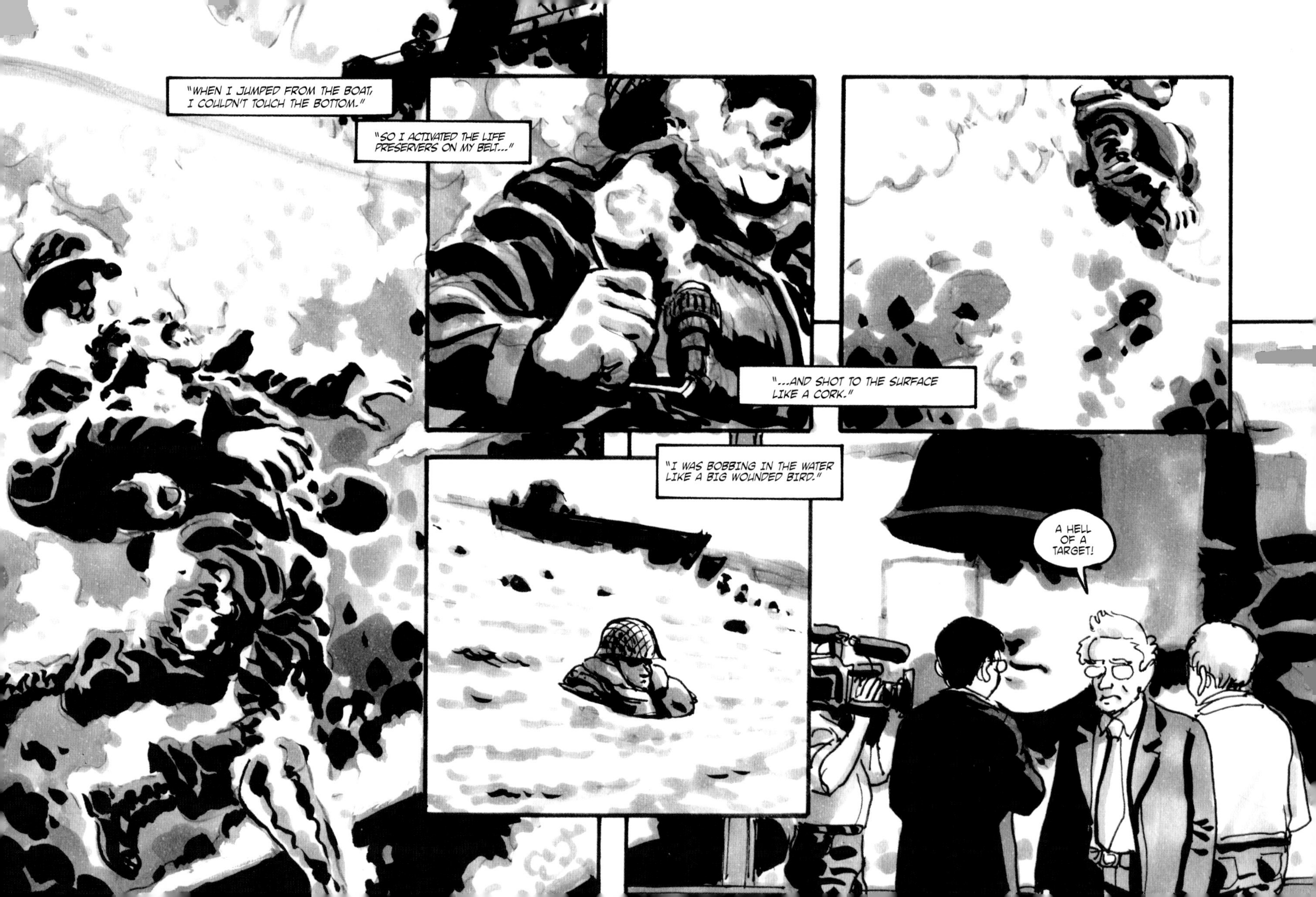
"WHEN I JUMPED FROM THE BOAT, I COULDN'T TOUCH THE BOTTOM."
"SO I ACTIVATED THE LIFE PRESERVERS ON MY BELT..."
"...AND SHOT TO THE SURFACE LIKE A CORK."
"I WAS BOBBING IN THE WATER LIKE A BIG WOUNDED BIRD."
A HELL OF A TARGET!

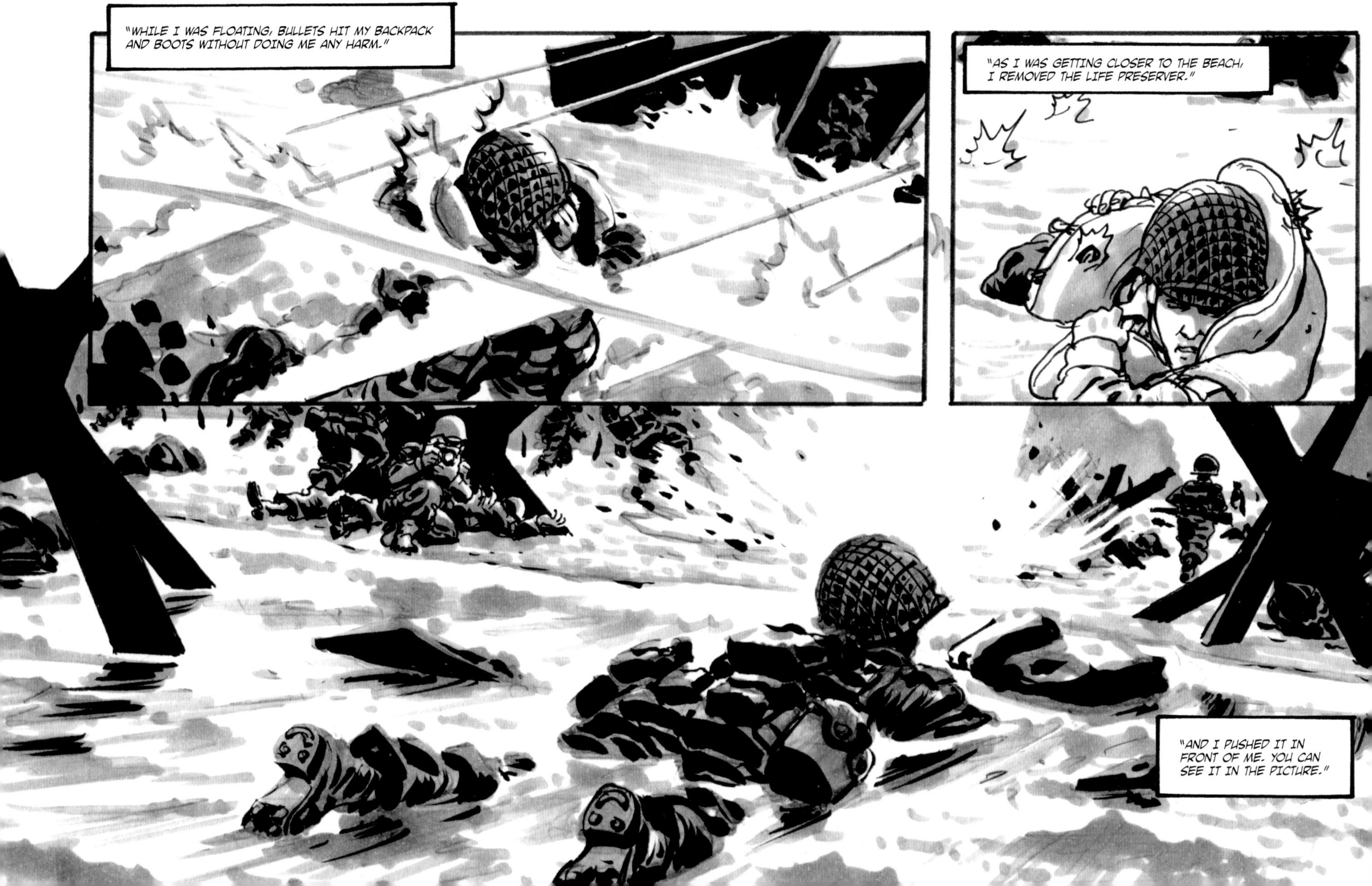
"WHILE I WAS FLOATING, BULLETS HIT MY BACKPACK AND BOOTS WITHOUT DOING ME ANY HARM."
"AS I WAS GETTING CLOSER TO THE BEACH, I REMOVED THE LIFE PRESERVER."
"AND I PUSHED IT IN FRONT OF ME. YOU CAN SEE IT IN THE PICTURE."

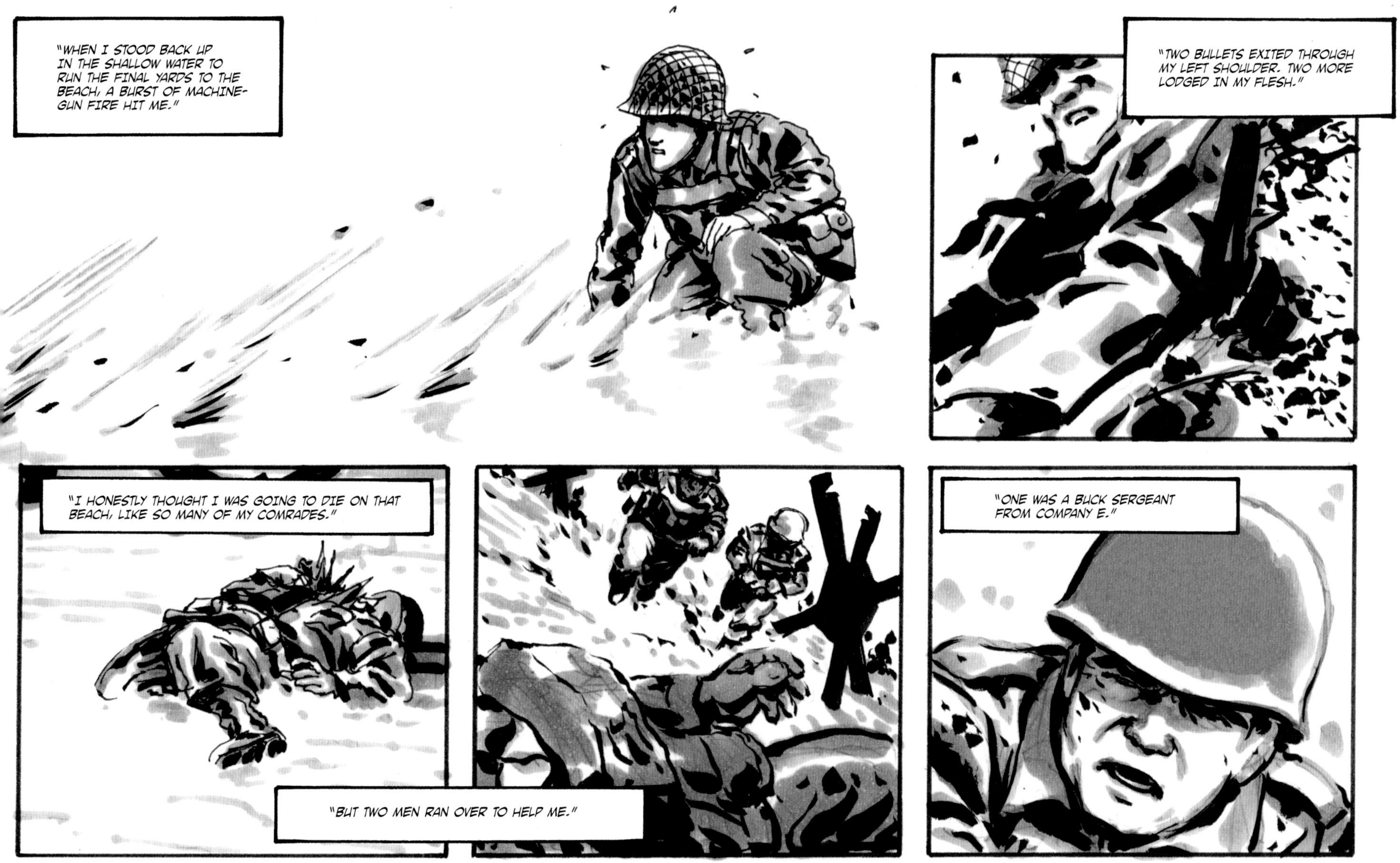
"WHEN I STOOD BACK UP IN THE SHALLOW WATER TO RUN THE FINAL YARDS TO THE BEACH, A BURST OF MACHINE-GUN FIRE HIT ME."
"TWO BULLETS EXITED THROUGH MY LEFT SHOULDER. TWO MORE LODGED IN MY FLESH."
"I HONESTLY THOUGHT I WAS GOING TO DIE ON THAT BEACH, LIKE SO MANY OF MY COMRADES."
"BUT TWO MEN RAN OVER TO HELP ME."
"ONE WAS A BUCK SERGEANT FROM COMPANY E."

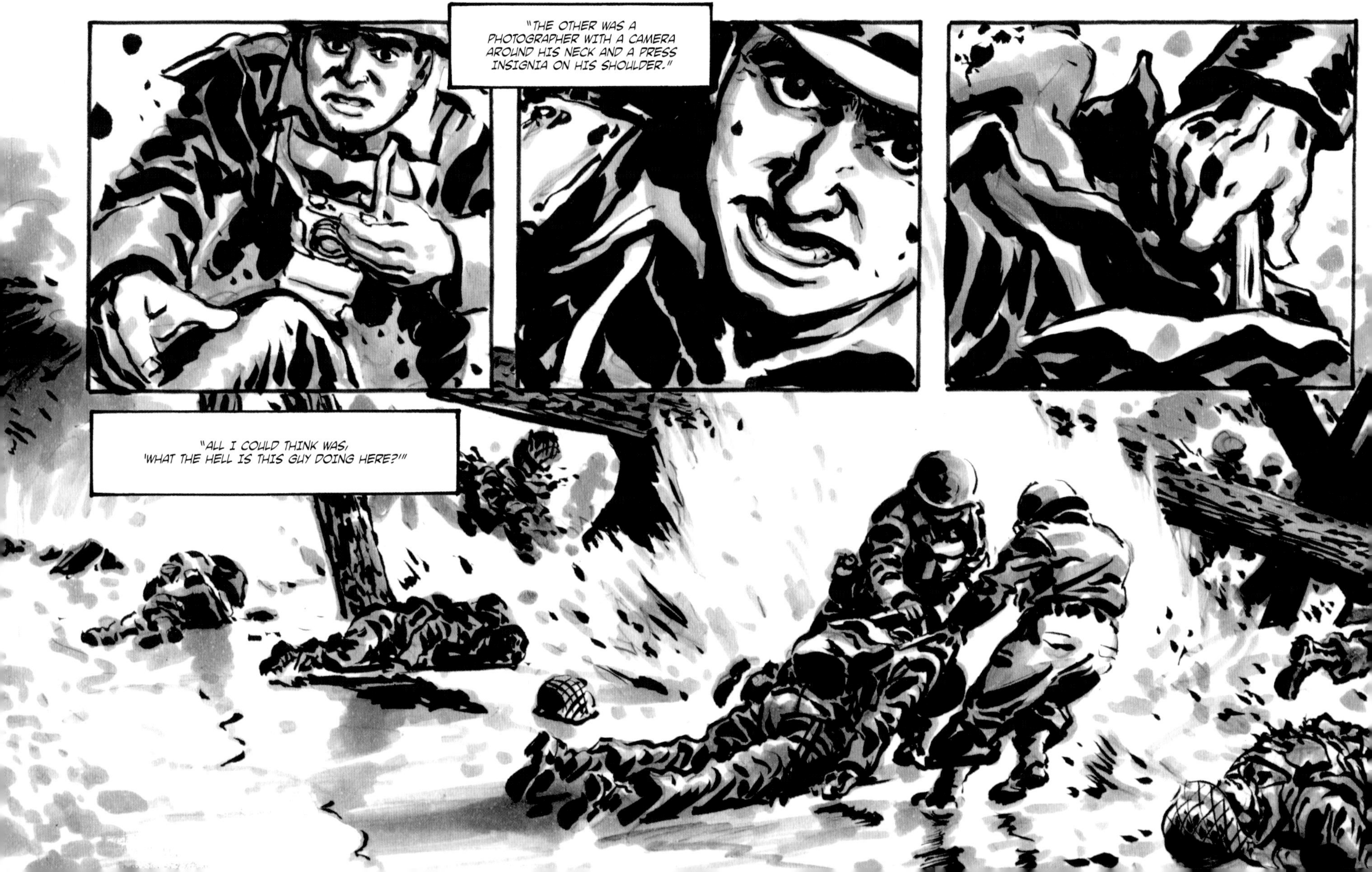
"THE OTHER WAS A PHOTOGRAPHER WITH A CAMERA AROUND HIS NECK AND A PRESS INSIGNIA ON HIS SHOULDER."
"ALL I COULD THINK WAS, 'WHAT THE HELL IS THIS GUY DOING HERE?'"

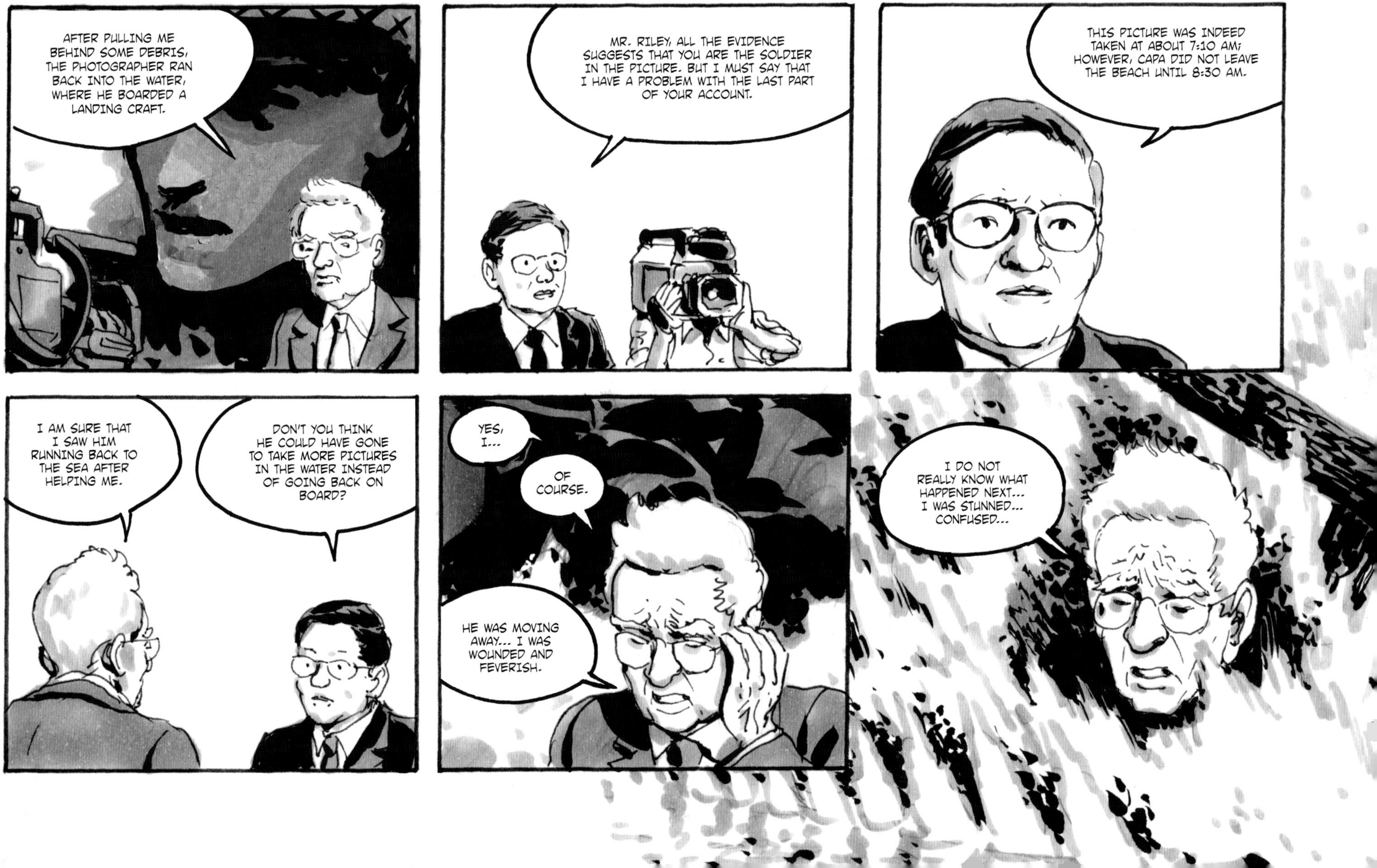
AFTER PULLING ME BEHIND SOME DEBRIS, THE PHOTOGRAPHER RAN BACK INTO THE WATER, WHERE HE BOARDED A LANDING CRAFT.
MR. RILEY, ALL THE EVIDENCE SUGGESTS THAT YOU ARE THE SOLDIER IN THE PICTURE. BUT I MUST SAY THAT I HAVE A PROBLEM WITH THE LAST PART OF YOUR ACCOUNT.
THIS PICTURE WAS INDEED TAKEN AT ABOUT 7:10 AM; HOWEVER, CAPA DID NOT LEAVE THE BEACH UNTIL 8:30 AM.
I AM SURE THAT I SAW HIM RUNNING BACK TO THE SEA AFTER HELPING ME.
DON'T YOU THINK HE COULD HAVE GONE TO TAKE MORE PICTURES IN THE WATER INSTEAD OF GOING BACK ON BOARD?
YES, I...
OF COURSE.
HE WAS MOVING AWAY... I WAS WOUNDED AND FEVERISH.
I DO NOT REALLY KNOW WHAT HAPPENED NEXT... I WAS STUNNED... CONFUSED...

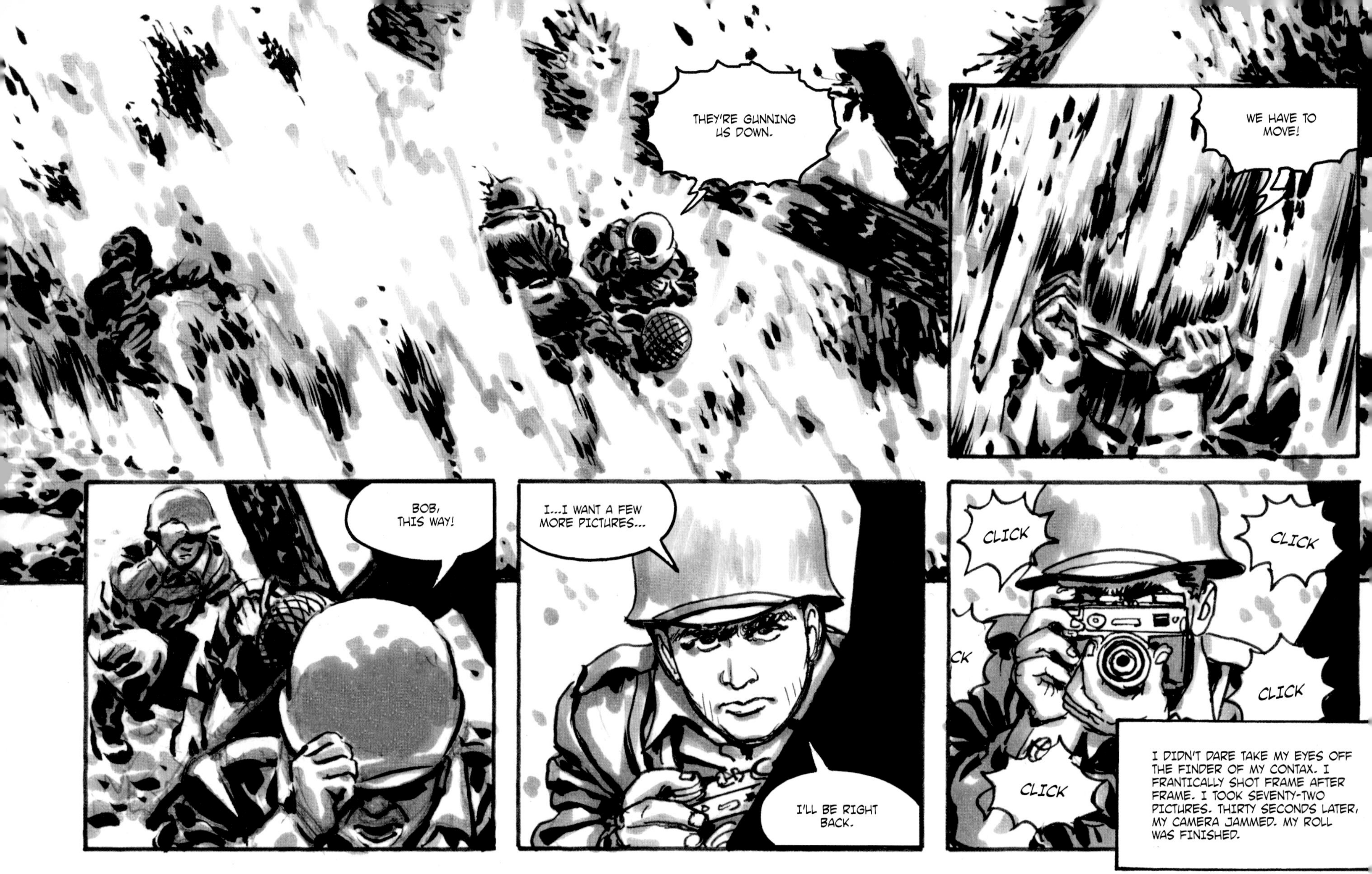

THEY'RE GUNNING US DOWN.
WE HAVE TO MOVE!
BOB, THIS WAY!
I...I WANT A FEW MORE PICTURES...
I'LL BE RIGHT BACK.
CLICK
CLICK
CK
CLICK
CLICK
I DIDN'T DARE TAKE MY EYES OFF THE FINDER OF MY CONTAX. I FRANTICALLY SHOT FRAME AFTER FRAME. I TOOK SEVENTY-TWO PICTURES. THIRTY SECONDS LATER, MY CAMERA JAMMED. MY ROLL WAS FINISHED.

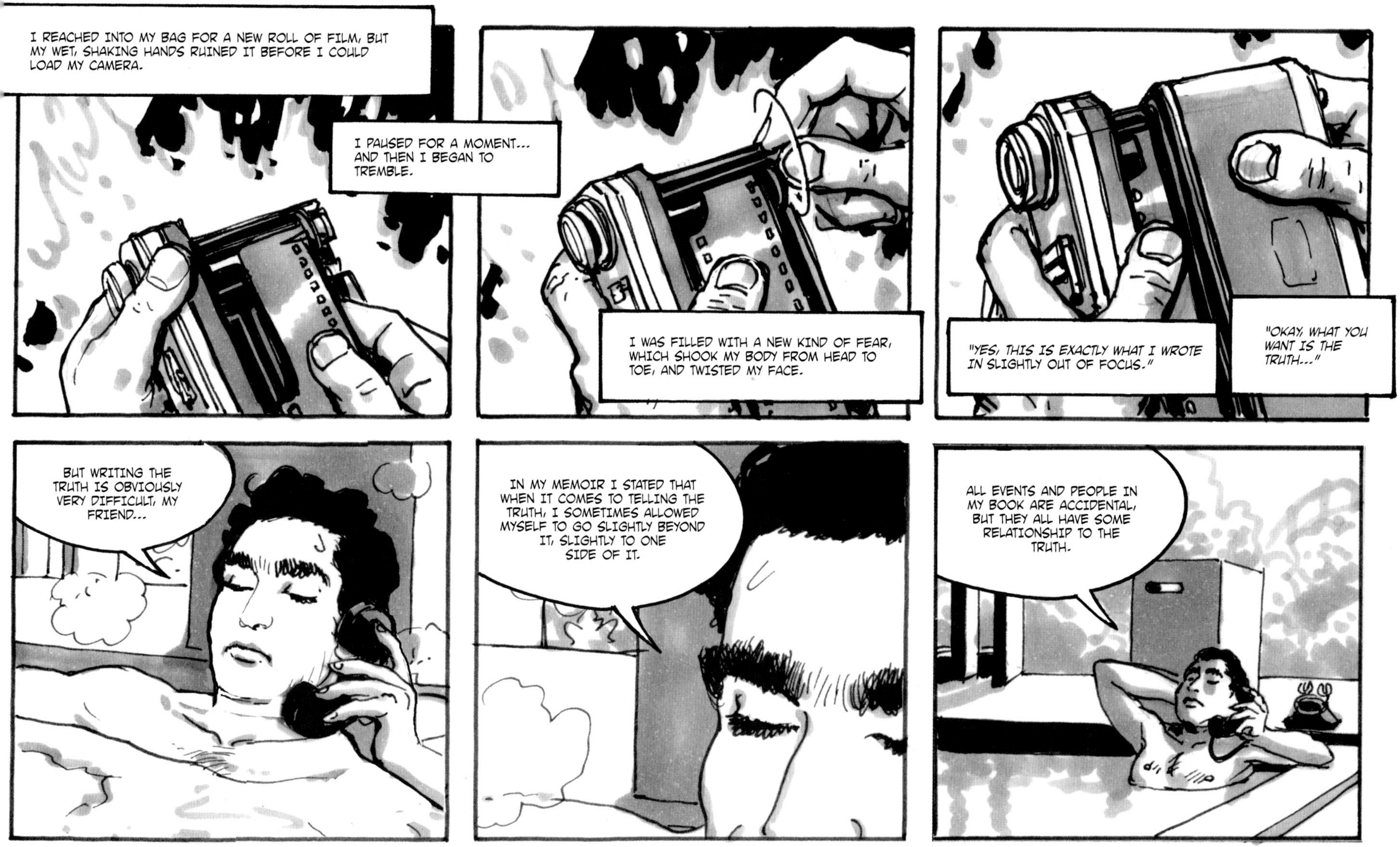
I REACHED INTO MY BAG FOR A NEW ROLL OF FILM, BUT MY WET, SHAKING HANDS RUINED IT BEFORE I COULD LOAD MY CAMERA.
I PAUSED FOR A MOMENT... AND THEN I BEGAN TO TREMBLE.
I WAS FILLED WITH A NEW KIND OF FEAR, WHICH SHOOK MY BODY FROM HEAD TO TOE, AND TWISTED MY FACE.
"YES, THIS IS EXACTLY WHAT I WROTE IN SLIGHTLY OUT OF FOCUS."
"OKAY, WHAT YOU WANT IS THE TRUTH..."
BUT WRITING THE TRUTH IS OBVIOUSLY VERY DIFFICULT, MY FRIEND...
IN MY MEMOIR I STATED THAT WHEN IT COMES TO TELLING THE TRUTH, I SOMETIMES ALLOWED MYSELF TO GO SLIGHTLY BEYOND IT, SLIGHTLY TO ONE SIDE OF IT.
ALL EVENTS AND PEOPLE IN MY BOOK ARE ACCIDENTAL, BUT THEY ALL HAVE SOME RELATIONSHIP TO THE TRUTH.

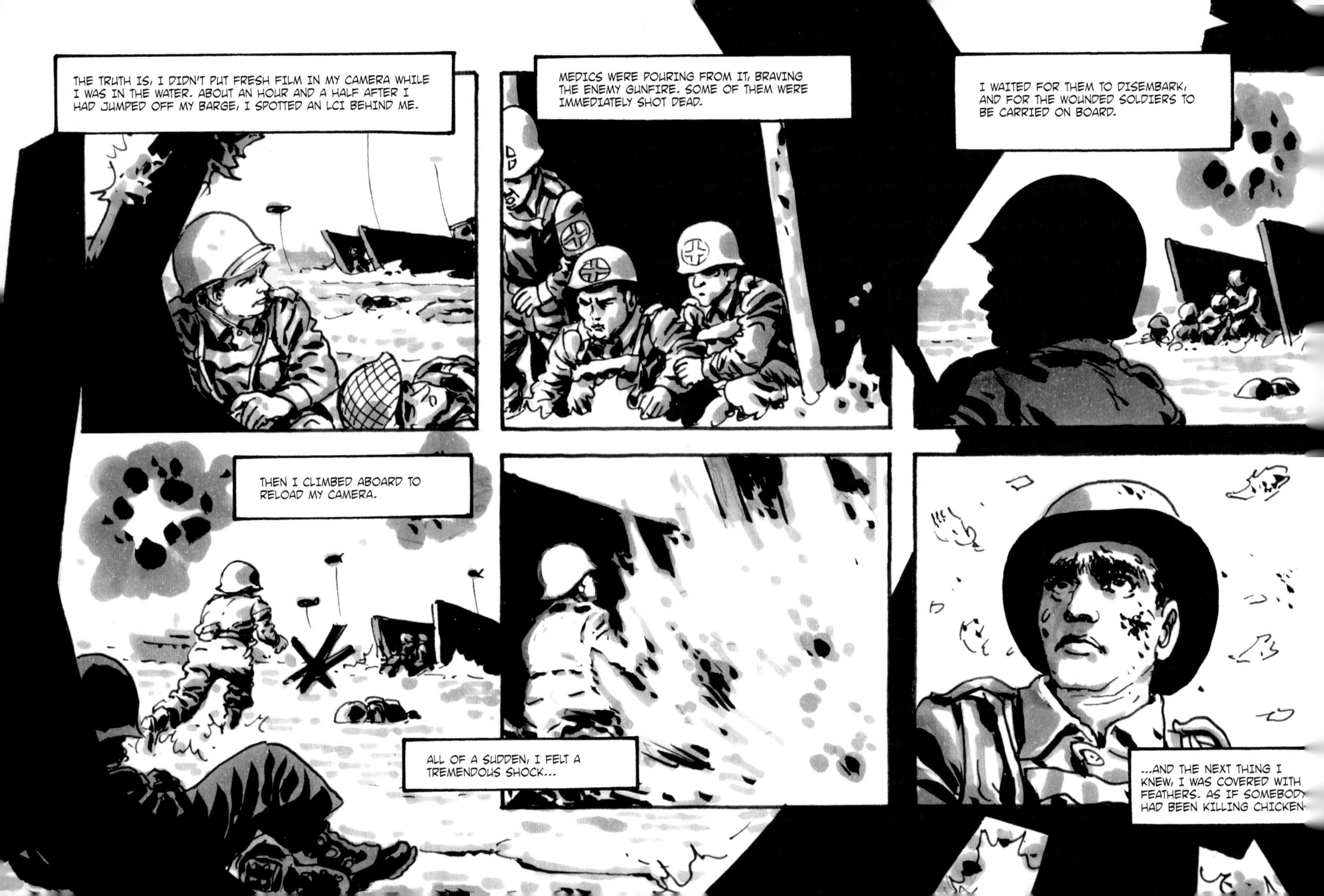
THE TRUTH IS, I DIDN'T PUT FRESH FILM IN MY CAMERA WHILE I WAS IN THE WATER. ABOUT AN HOUR AND A HALF AFTER I HAD JUMPED OFF MY BARGE, I SPOTTED AN LCI BEHIND ME.
MEDICS WERE POURING FROM IT, BRAVING THE ENEMY GUNFIRE. SOME OF THEM WERE IMMEDIATELY SHOT DEAD.
I WAITED FOR THEM TO DISEMBARK, AND FOR THE WOUNDED SOLDIERS TO BE CARRIED ON BOARD.
THEN I CLIMBED ABOARD TO RELOAD MY CAMERA.
ALL OF A SUDDEN, I FELT A TREMENDOUS SHOCK...
...AND THE NEXT THING I KNEW, I WAS COVERED WITH FEATHERS. AS IF SOMEBODY HAD BEEN KILLING CHICKEN

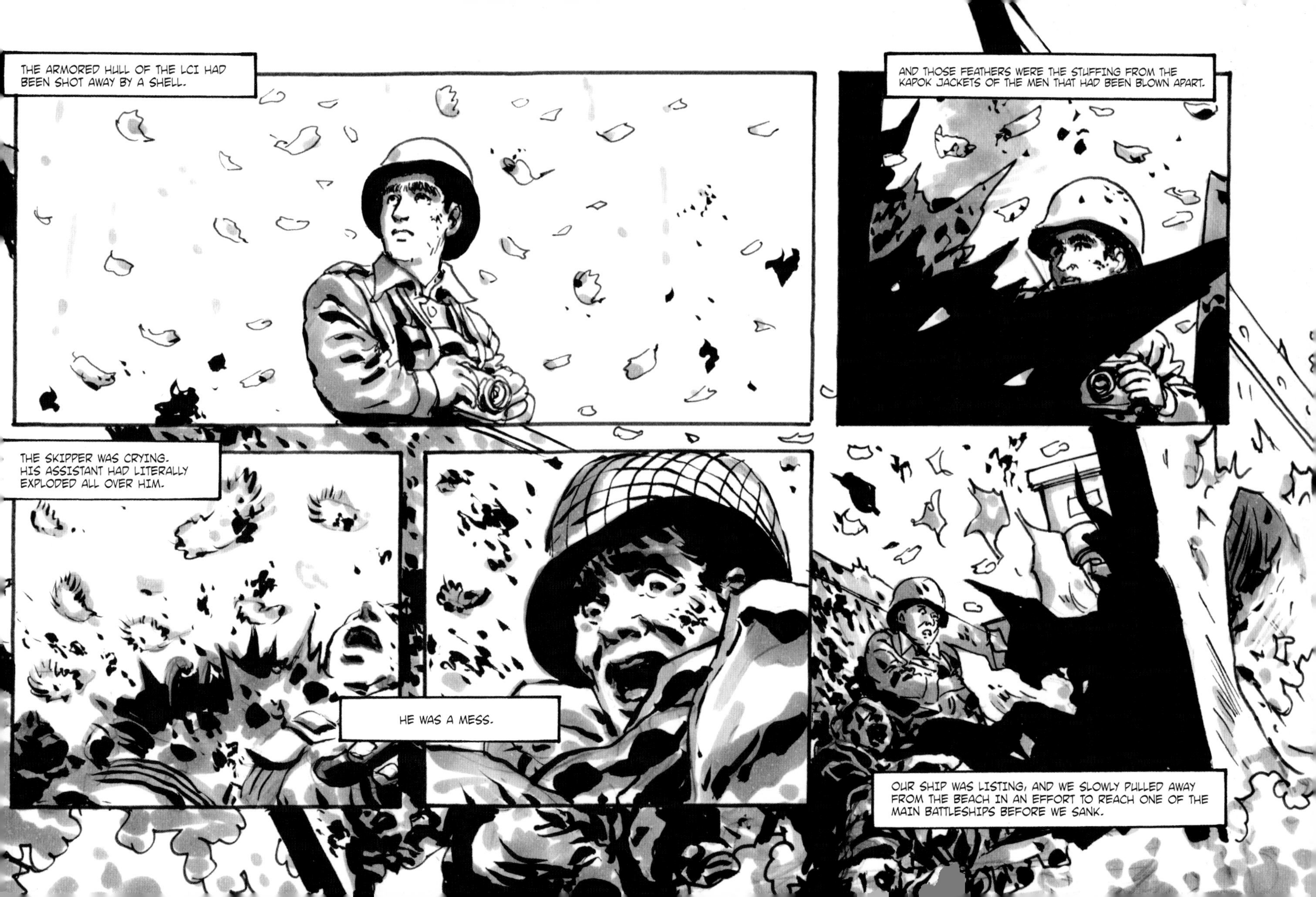
THE ARMORED HULL OF THE LCI HAD BEEN SHOT AWAY BY A SHELL.
AND THOSE FEATHERS WERE THE STUFFING FROM THE KAPOK JACKETS OF THE MEN THAT HAD BEEN BLOWN APART.
THE SKIPPER WAS CRYING. HIS ASSISTANT HAD LITERALLY EXPLODED ALL OVER HIM.
HE WAS A MESS.
OUR SHIP WAS LISTING, AND WE SLOWLY PULLED AWAY FROM THE BEACH IN AN EFFORT TO REACH ONE OF THE MAIN BATTLESHIPS BEFORE WE SANK.

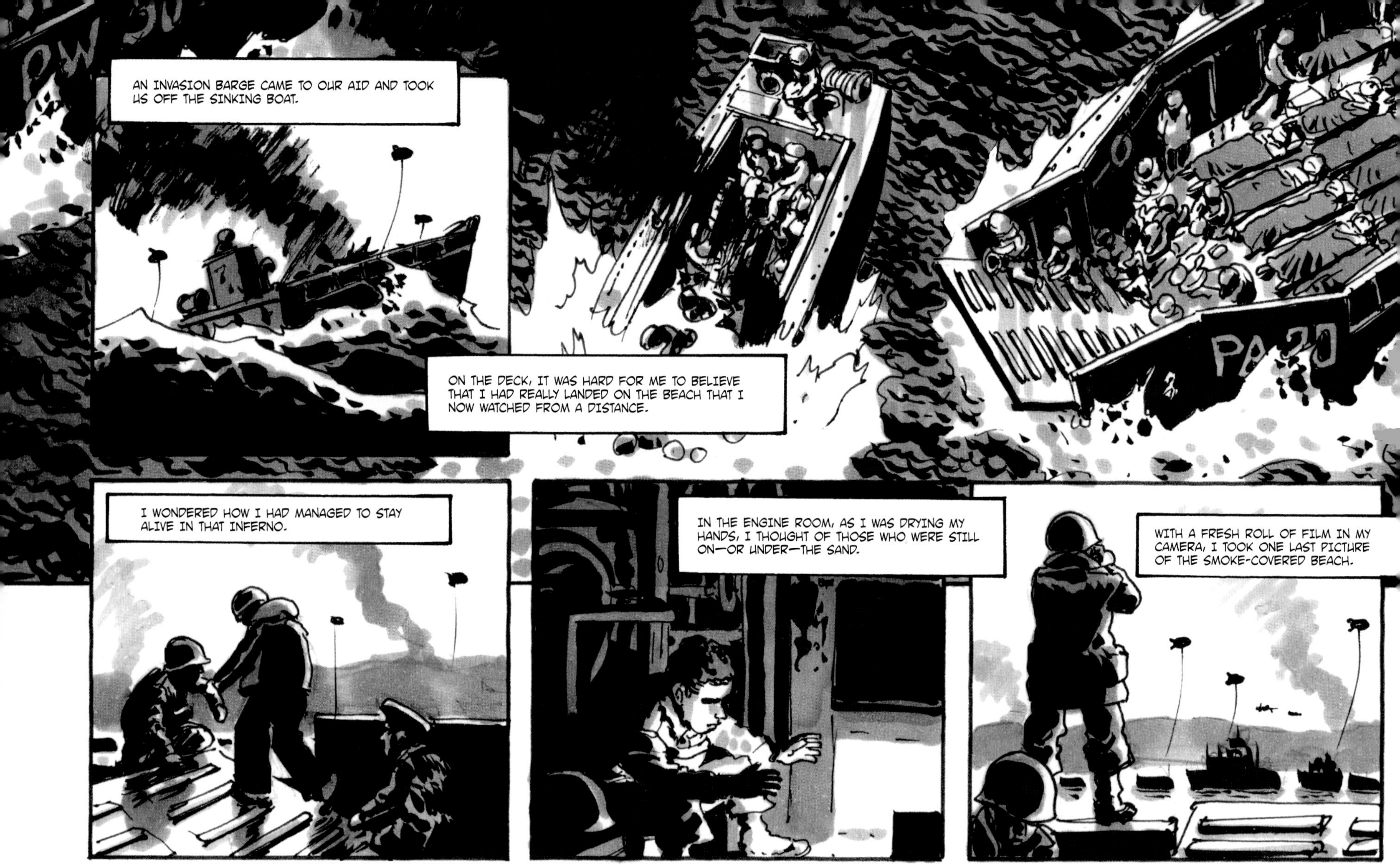
AN INVASION BARGE CAME TO OUR AID AND TOOK US OFF THE SINKING BOAT.
ON THE DECK, IT WAS HARD FOR ME TO BELIEVE THAT I HAD REALLY LANDED ON THE BEACH THAT I NOW WATCHED FROM A DISTANCE.
PA 30
I WONDERED HOW I HAD MANAGED TO STAY ALIVE IN THAT INFERNO.
IN THE ENGINE ROOM, AS I WAS DRYING MY HANDS, I THOUGHT OF THOSE WHO WERE STILL ON—OR UNDER—THE SAND.
WITH A FRESH ROLL OF FILM IN MY CAMERA, I TOOK ONE LAST PICTURE OF THE SMOKE-COVERED BEACH.

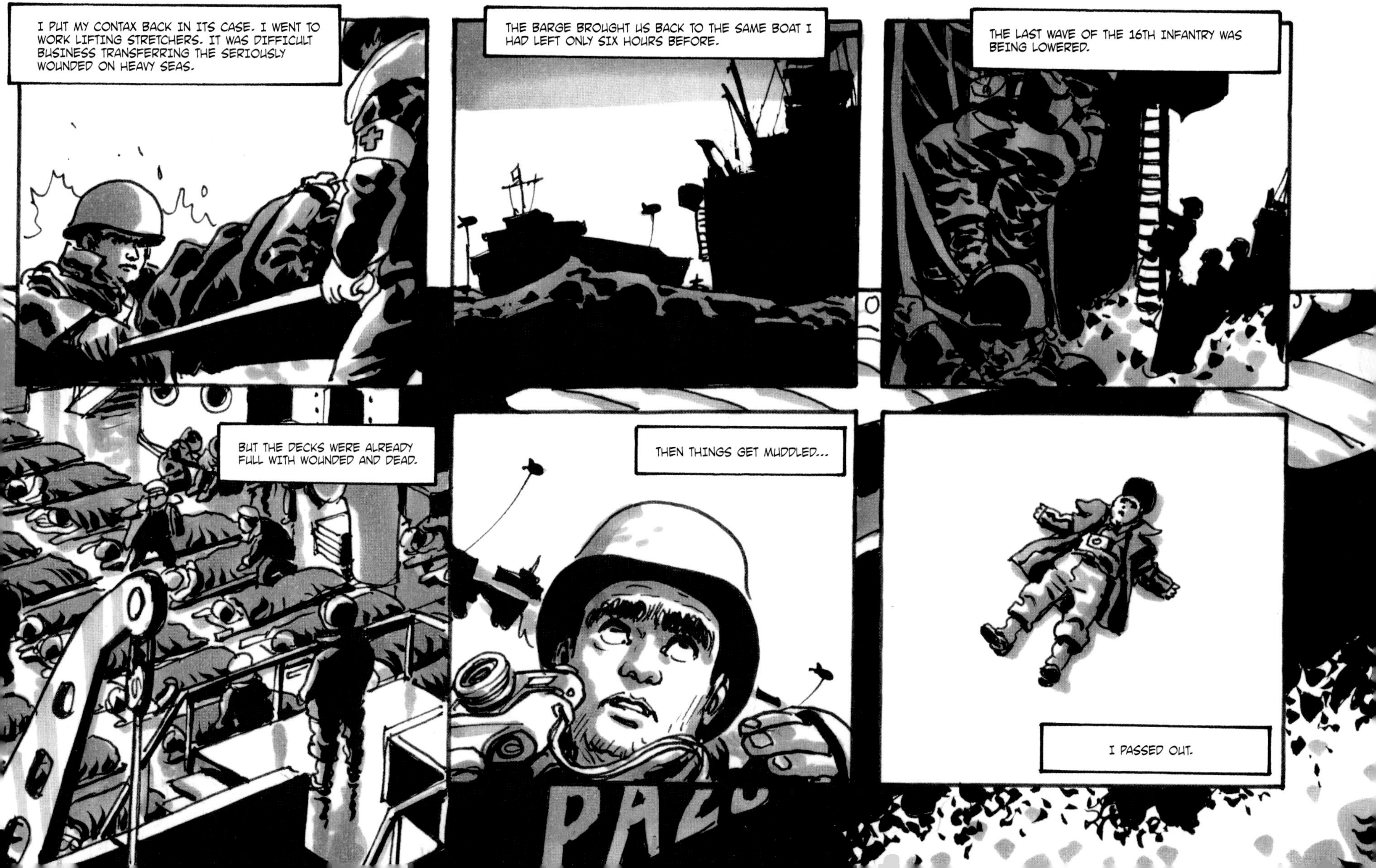
I PUT MY CONTAX BACK IN ITS CASE. I WENT TO WORK LIFTING STRETCHERS. IT WAS DIFFICULT BUSINESS TRANSFERRING THE SERIOUSLY WOUNDED ON HEAVY SEAS.
THE BARGE BROUGHT US BACK TO THE SAME BOAT I HAD LEFT ONLY SIX HOURS BEFORE.
THE LAST WAVE OF THE 16TH INFANTRY WAS BEING LOWERED.
BUT THE DECKS WERE ALREADY FULL WITH WOUNDED AND DEAD.
THEN THINGS GET MUDDLED...
I PASSED OUT.

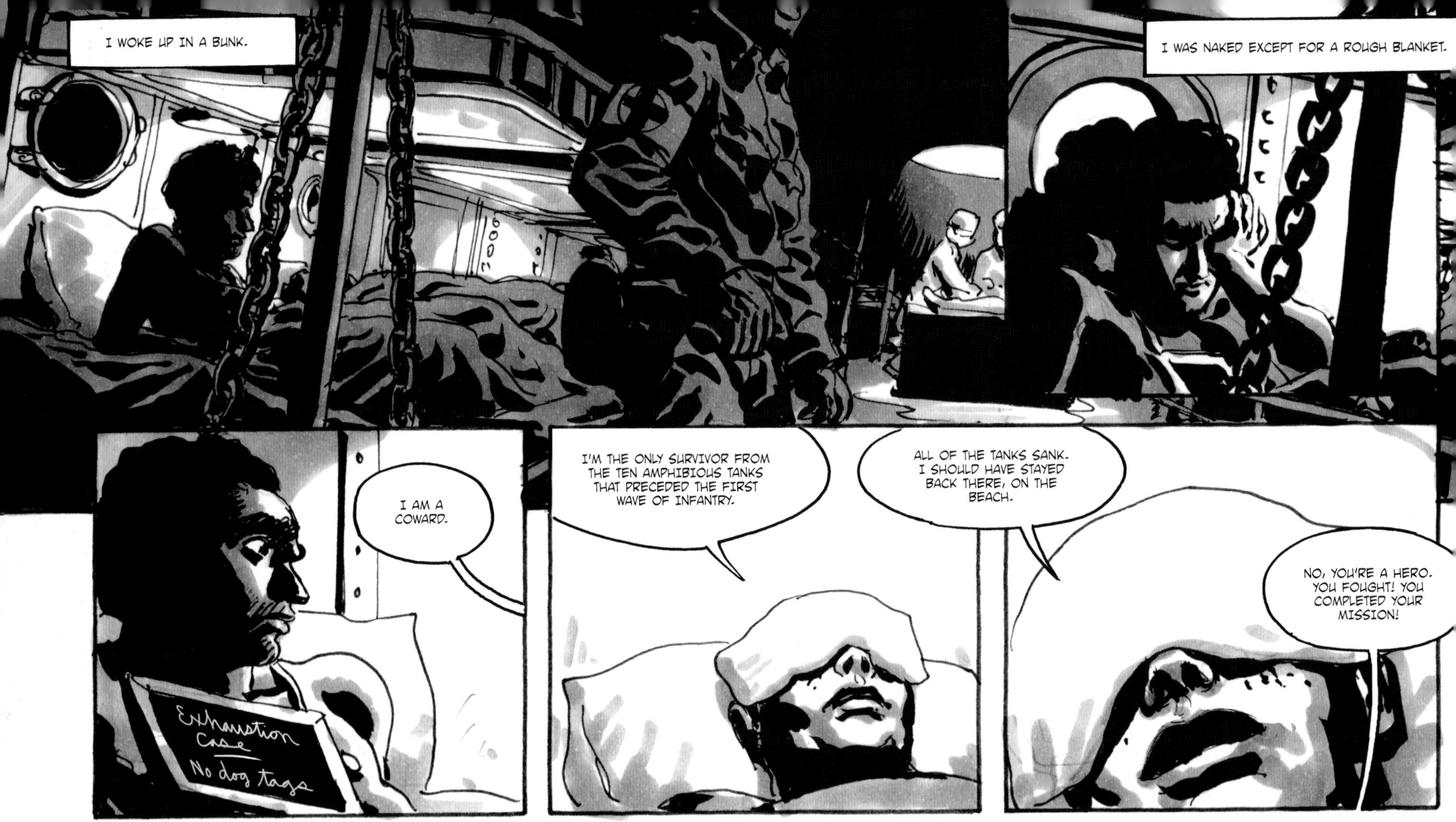
I WOKE UP IN A BUNK.
I WAS NAKED EXCEPT FOR A ROUGH BLANKET.
I AM A COWARD.
Exhaustion Case
No dog tags
I'M THE ONLY SURVIVOR FROM THE TEN AMPHIBIOUS TANKS THAT PRECEDED THE FIRST WAVE OF INFANTRY.
ALL OF THE TANKS SANK. I SHOULD HAVE STAYED BACK THERE, ON THE BEACH.
NO, YOU'RE A HERO. YOU FOUGHT! YOU COMPLETED YOUR MISSION!

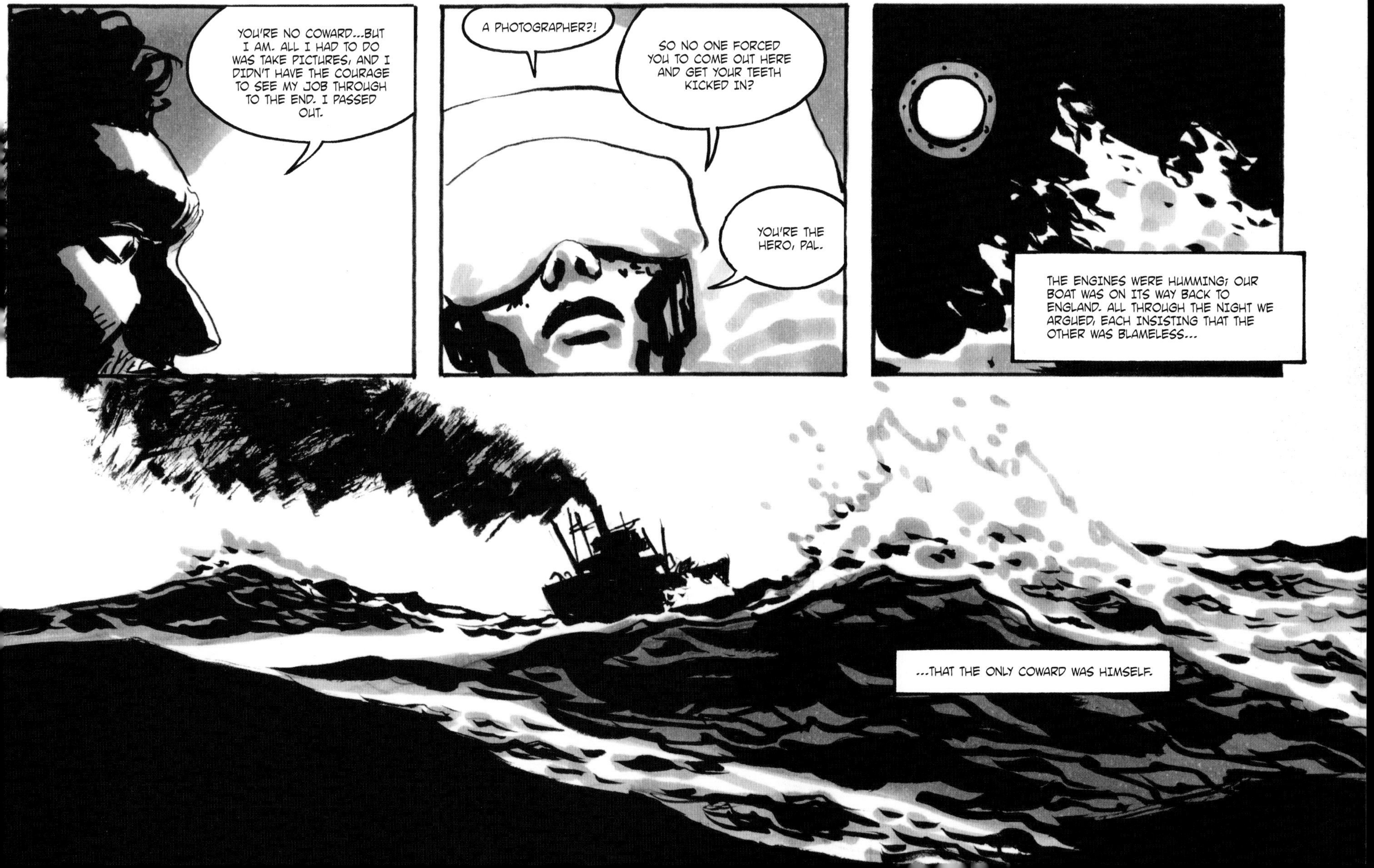
YOU'RE NO COWARD...BUT I AM. ALL I HAD TO DO WAS TAKE PICTURES, AND I DIDN'T HAVE THE COURAGE TO SEE MY JOB THROUGH TO THE END. I PASSED OUT.
A PHOTOGRAPHER?!
SO NO ONE FORCED YOU TO COME OUT HERE AND GET YOUR TEETH KICKED IN?
YOU'RE THE HERO, PAL.
THE ENGINES WERE HUMMING; OUR BOAT WAS ON ITS WAY BACK TO ENGLAND. ALL THROUGH THE NIGHT WE ARGUED, EACH INSISTING THAT THE OTHER WAS BLAMELESS...
...THAT THE ONLY COWARD WAS HIMSELF.

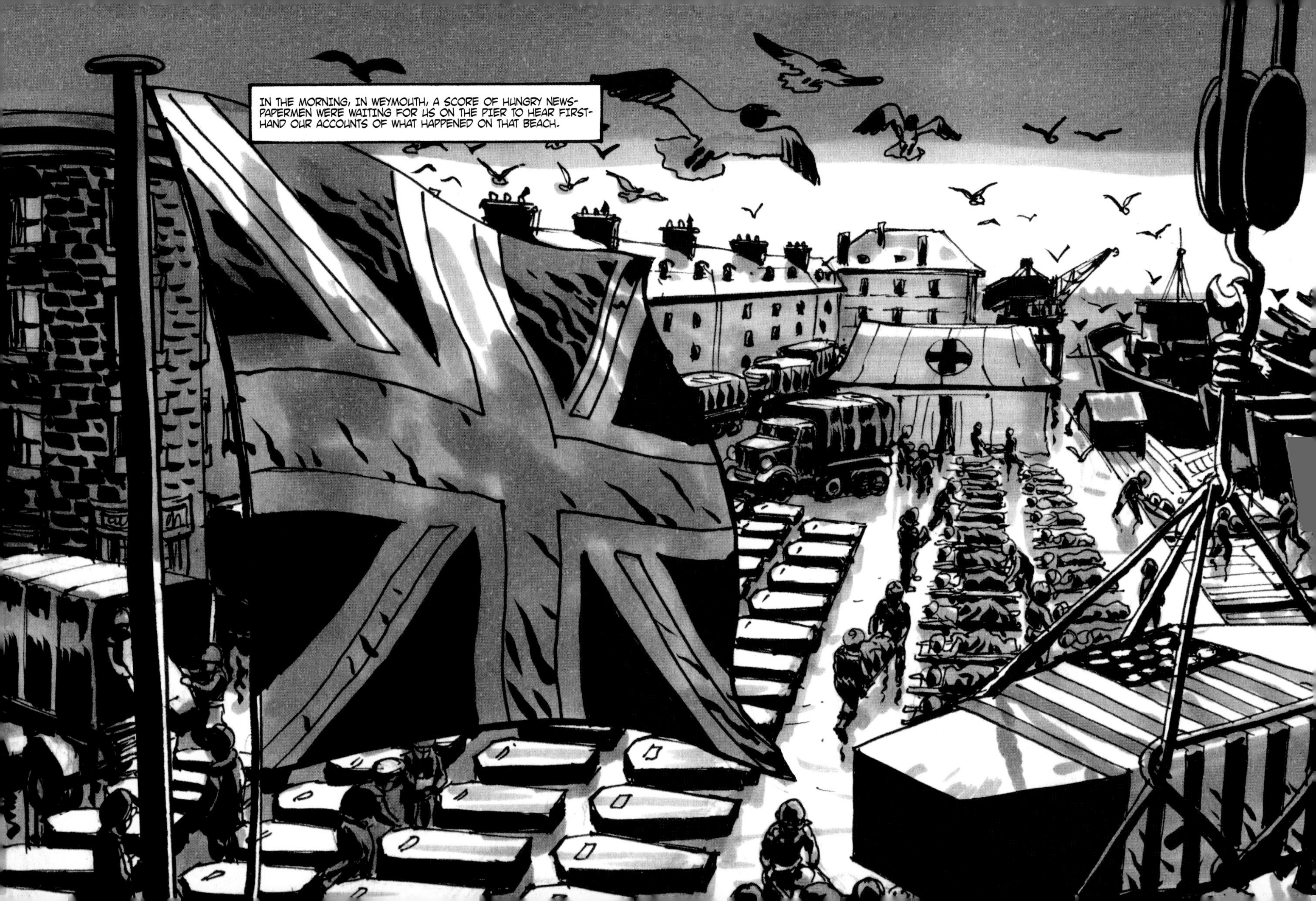
IN THE MORNING, IN WEYMOUTH, A SCORE OF HUNGRY NEWS-PAPERMEN WERE WAITING FOR US ON THE PIER TO HEAR FIRST-HAND OUR ACCOUNTS OF WHAT HAPPENED ON THAT BEACH.

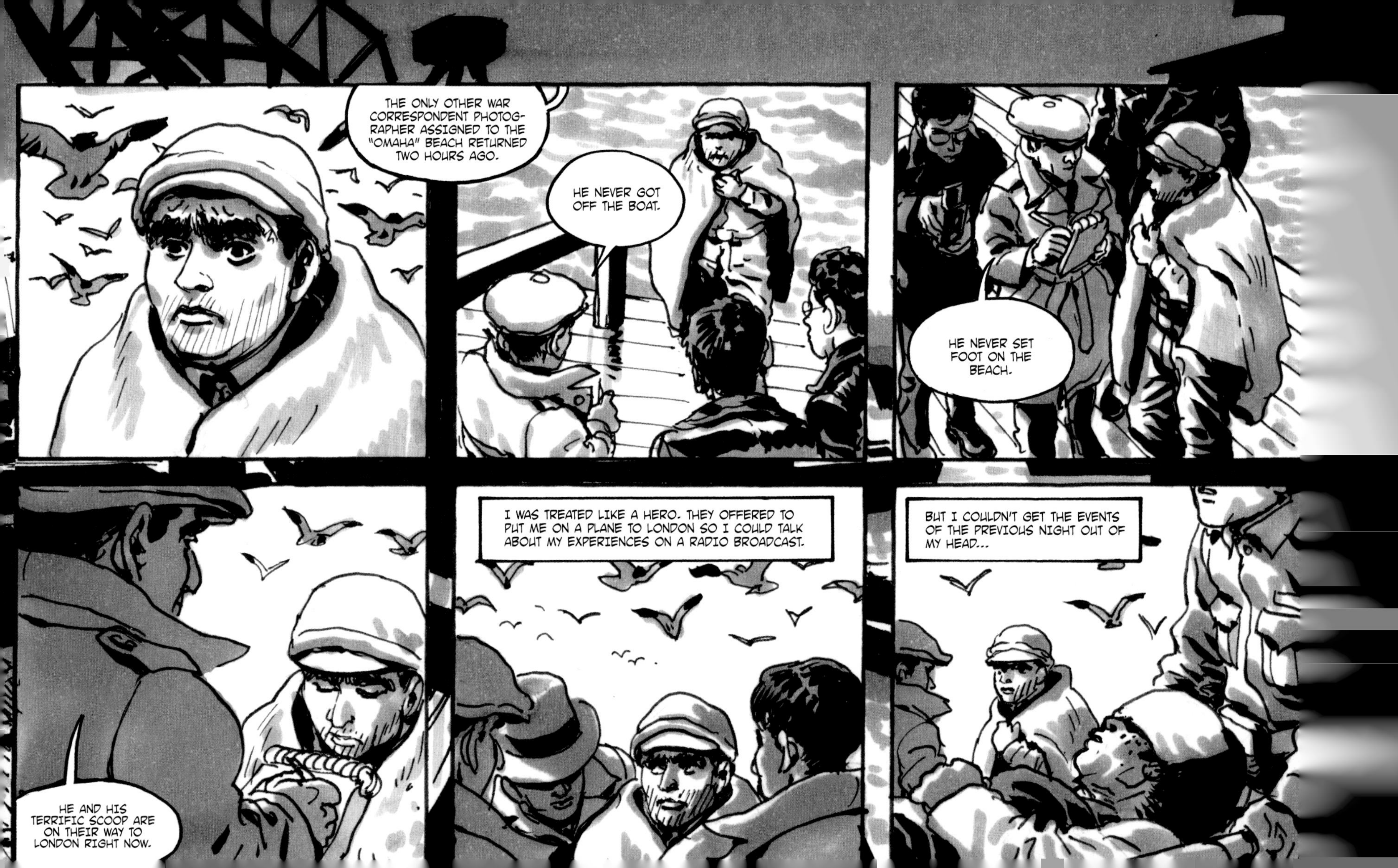
THE ONLY OTHER WAR CORRESPONDENT PHOTOG-RAPHER ASSIGNED TO THE "OMAHA" BEACH RETURNED TWO HOURS AGO.
HE NEVER GOT OFF THE BOAT.
HE NEVER SET FOOT ON THE BEACH.
HE AND HIS TERRIFIC SCOOP ARE ON THEIR WAY TO LONDON RIGHT NOW.
I WAS TREATED LIKE A HERO. THEY OFFERED TO PUT ME ON A PLANE TO LONDON SO I COULD TALK ABOUT MY EXPERIENCES ON A RADIO BROADCAST.
BUT I COULDN'T GET THE EVENTS OF THE PREVIOUS NIGHT OUT OF MY HEAD...

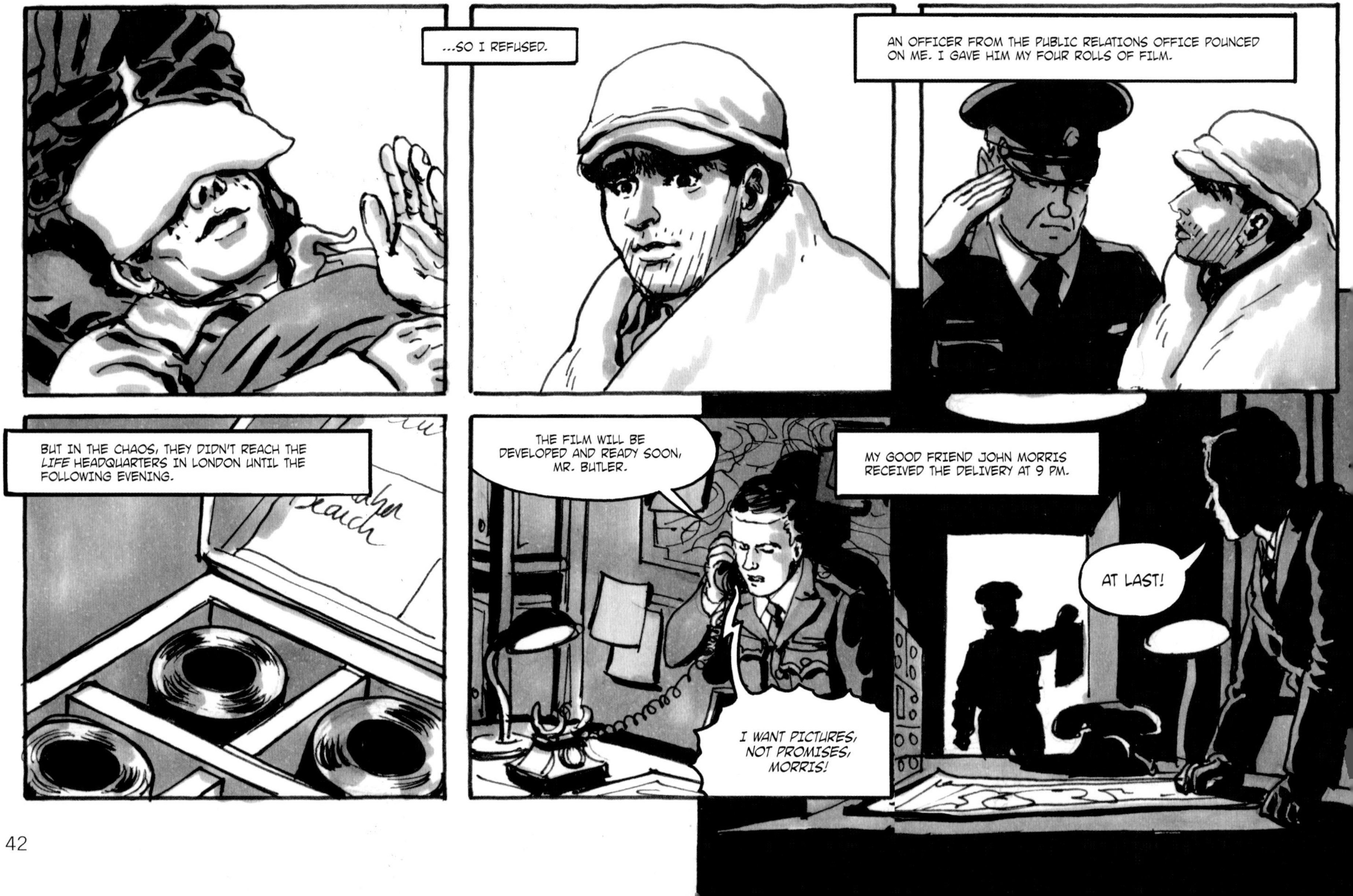

...SO I REFUSED.
AN OFFICER FROM THE PUBLIC RELATIONS OFFICE POUNCED ON ME. I GAVE HIM MY FOUR ROLLS OF FILM.
BUT IN THE CHAOS, THEY DIDN'T REACH THE *LIFE* HEADQUARTERS IN LONDON UNTIL THE FOLLOWING EVENING.
THE FILM WILL BE DEVELOPED AND READY SOON, MR. BUTLER.
I WANT PICTURES, NOT PROMISES, MORRIS!
MY GOOD FRIEND JOHN MORRIS RECEIVED THE DELIVERY AT 9 PM.
AT LAST!

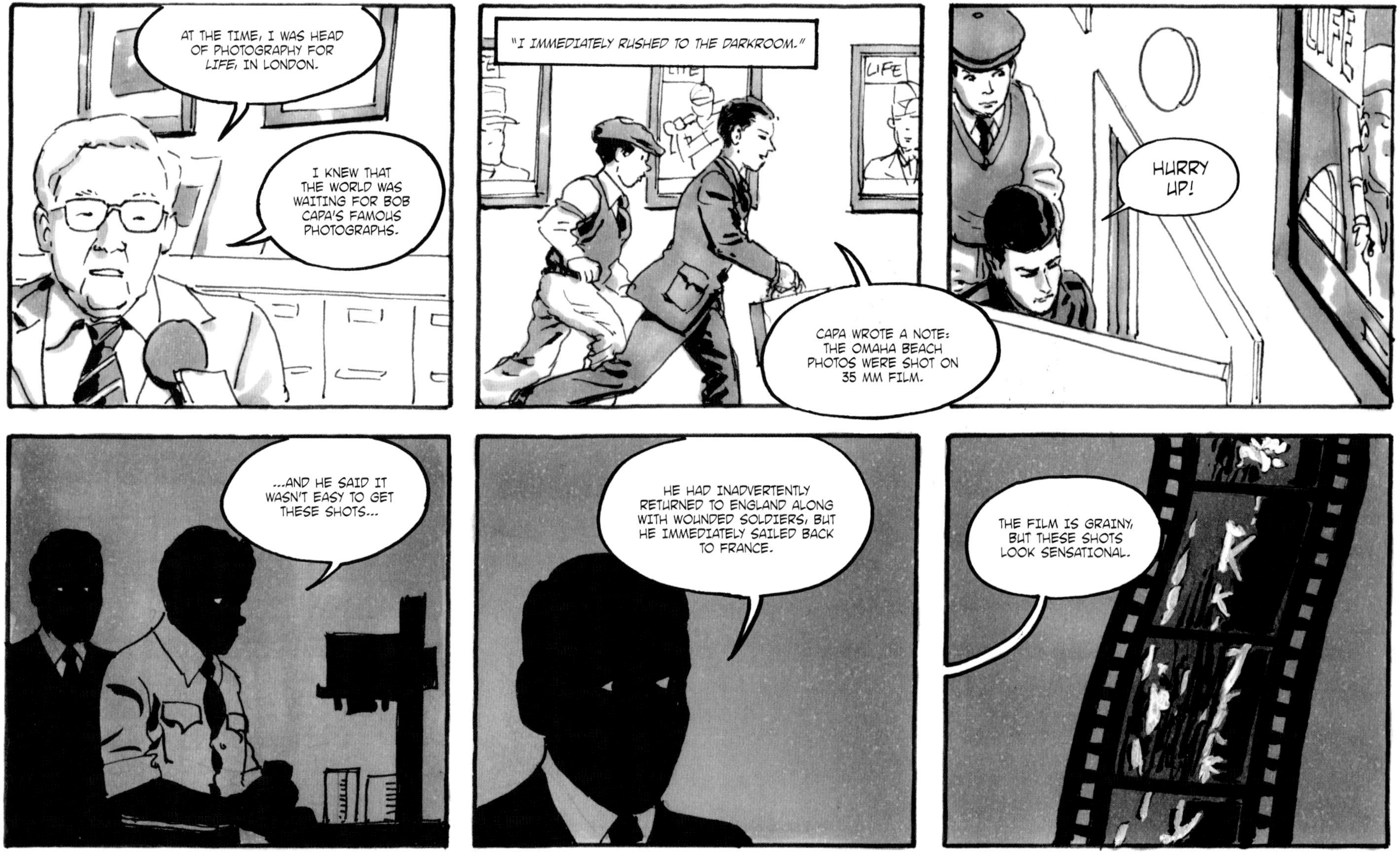
AT THE TIME, I WAS HEAD OF PHOTOGRAPHY FOR *LIFE*, IN LONDON.
I KNEW THAT THE WORLD WAS WAITING FOR BOB CAPA'S FAMOUS PHOTOGRAPHS.
"I IMMEDIATELY RUSHED TO THE DARKROOM."
LIFE
CAPA WROTE A NOTE: THE OMAHA BEACH PHOTOS WERE SHOT ON 35 MM FILM.
HURRY UP!
LIFE
...AND HE SAID IT WASN'T EASY TO GET THESE SHOTS...
HE HAD INADVERTENTLY RETURNED TO ENGLAND ALONG WITH WOUNDED SOLDIERS, BUT HE IMMEDIATELY SAILED BACK TO FRANCE.
THE FILM IS GRAINY, BUT THESE SHOTS LOOK SENSATIONAL.

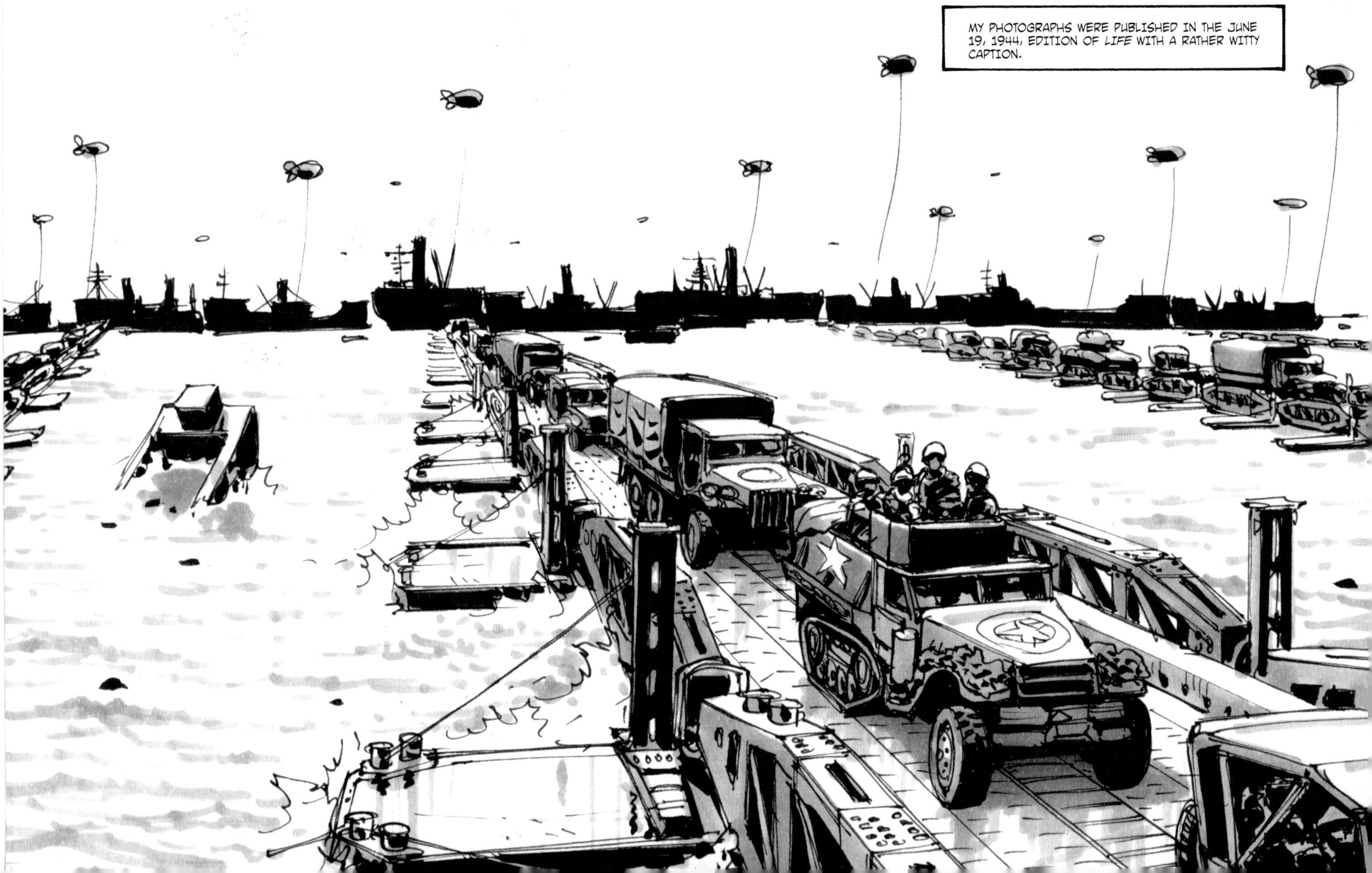
MY PHOTOGRAPHS WERE PUBLISHED IN THE JUNE 19, 1944, EDITION OF *LIFE* WITH A RATHER WITTY CAPTION.

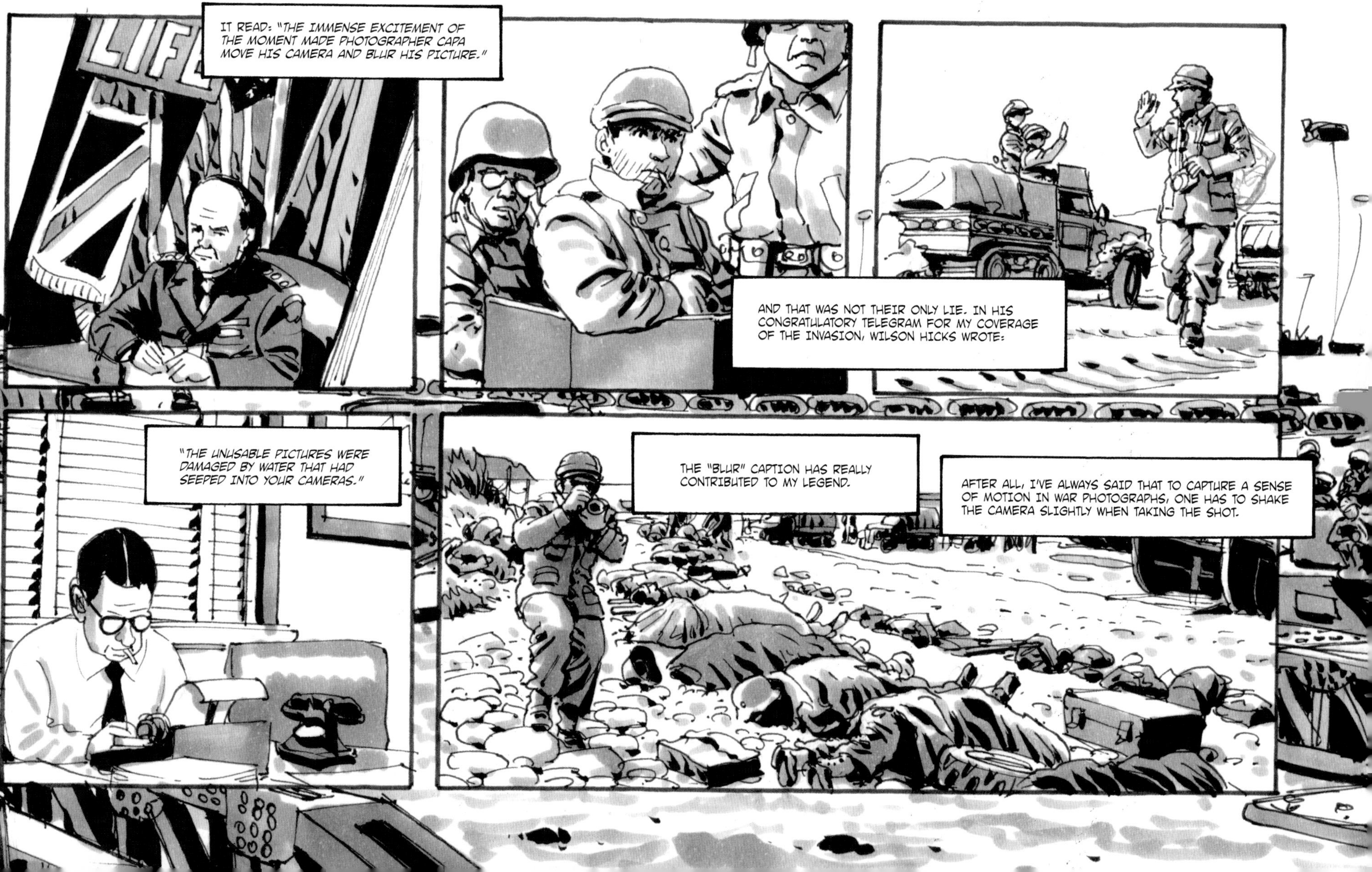
IT READ: "THE IMMENSE EXCITEMENT OF THE MOMENT MADE PHOTOGRAPHER CAPA MOVE HIS CAMERA AND BLUR HIS PICTURE."
AND THAT WAS NOT THEIR ONLY LIE. IN HIS CONGRATULATORY TELEGRAM FOR MY COVERAGE OF THE INVASION, WILSON HICKS WROTE:
"THE UNUSABLE PICTURES WERE DAMAGED BY WATER THAT HAD SEEPED INTO YOUR CAMERAS."
THE "BLUR" CAPTION HAS REALLY CONTRIBUTED TO MY LEGEND.
AFTER ALL, I'VE ALWAYS SAID THAT TO CAPTURE A SENSE OF MOTION IN WAR PHOTOGRAPHS, ONE HAS TO SHAKE THE CAMERA SLIGHTLY WHEN TAKING THE SHOT.

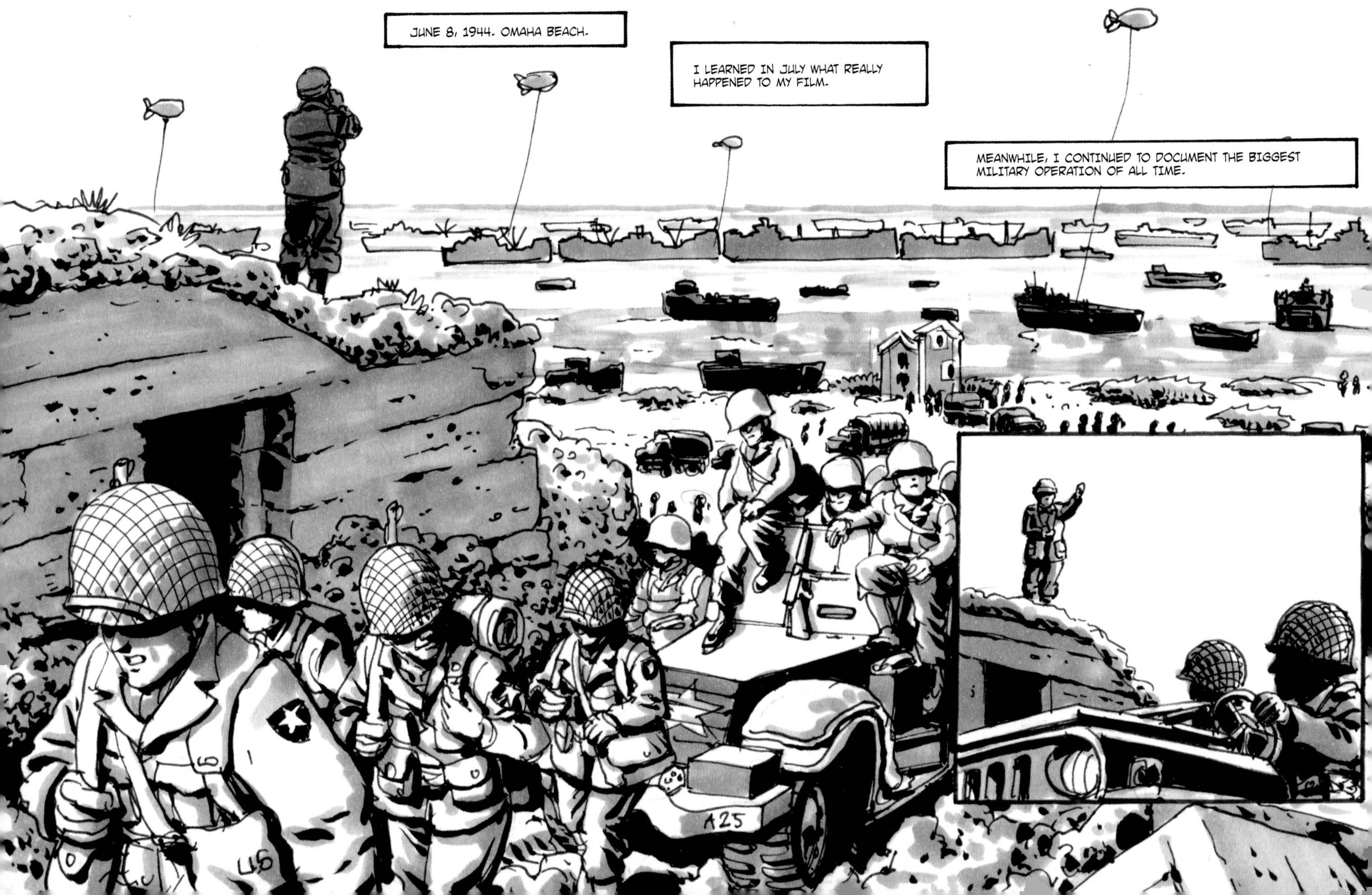
JUNE 8, 1944. OMAHA BEACH.
I LEARNED IN JULY WHAT REALLY HAPPENED TO MY FILM.
MEANWHILE, I CONTINUED TO DOCUMENT THE BIGGEST MILITARY OPERATION OF ALL TIME.
A25

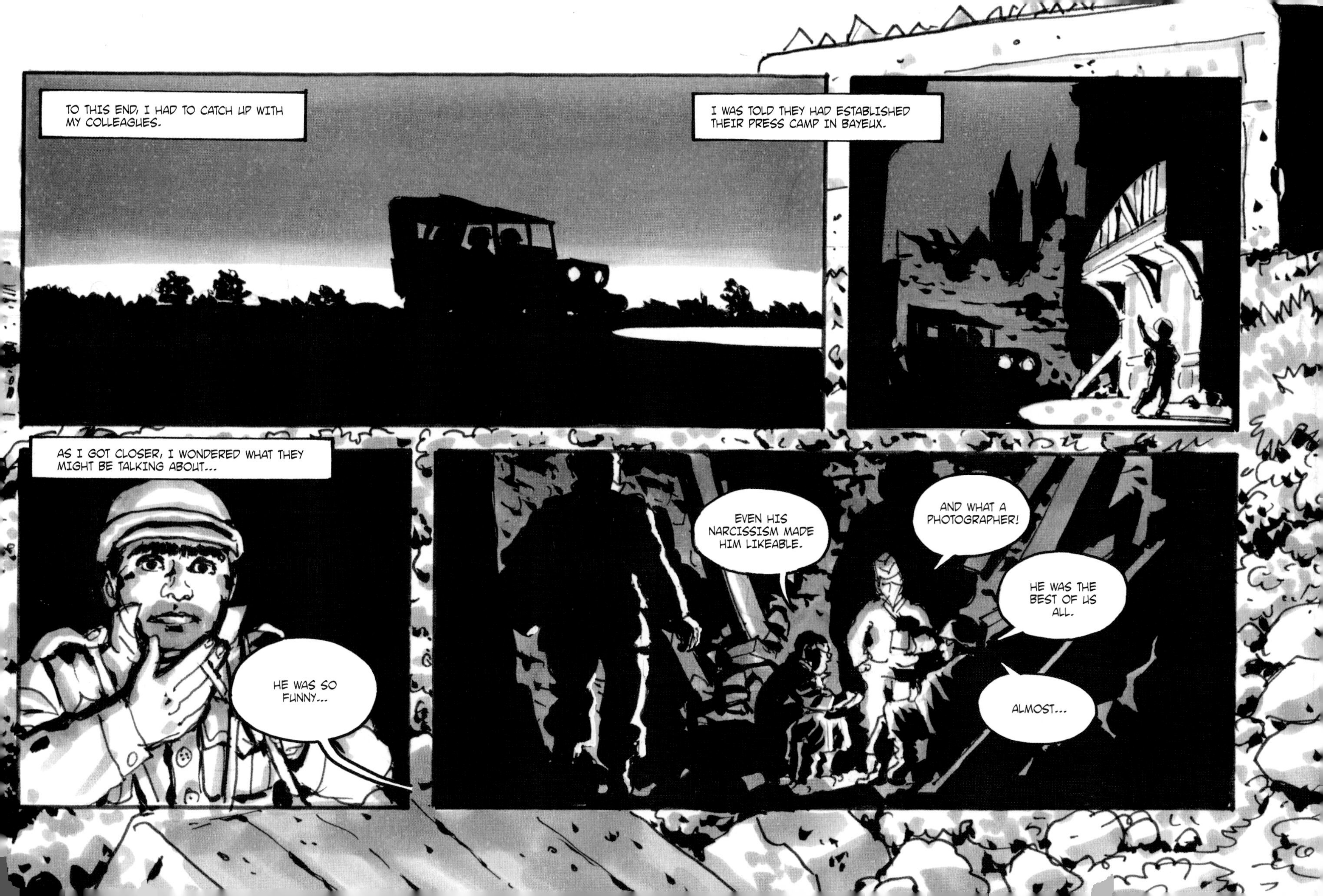
TO THIS END, I HAD TO CATCH UP WITH MY COLLEAGUES.
I WAS TOLD THEY HAD ESTABLISHED THEIR PRESS CAMP IN BAYEUX.
AS I GOT CLOSER, I WONDERED WHAT THEY MIGHT BE TALKING ABOUT...
HE WAS SO FUNNY...
EVEN HIS NARCISSISM MADE HIM LIKEABLE.
AND WHAT A PHOTOGRAPHER!
HE WAS THE BEST OF US ALL.
ALMOST...

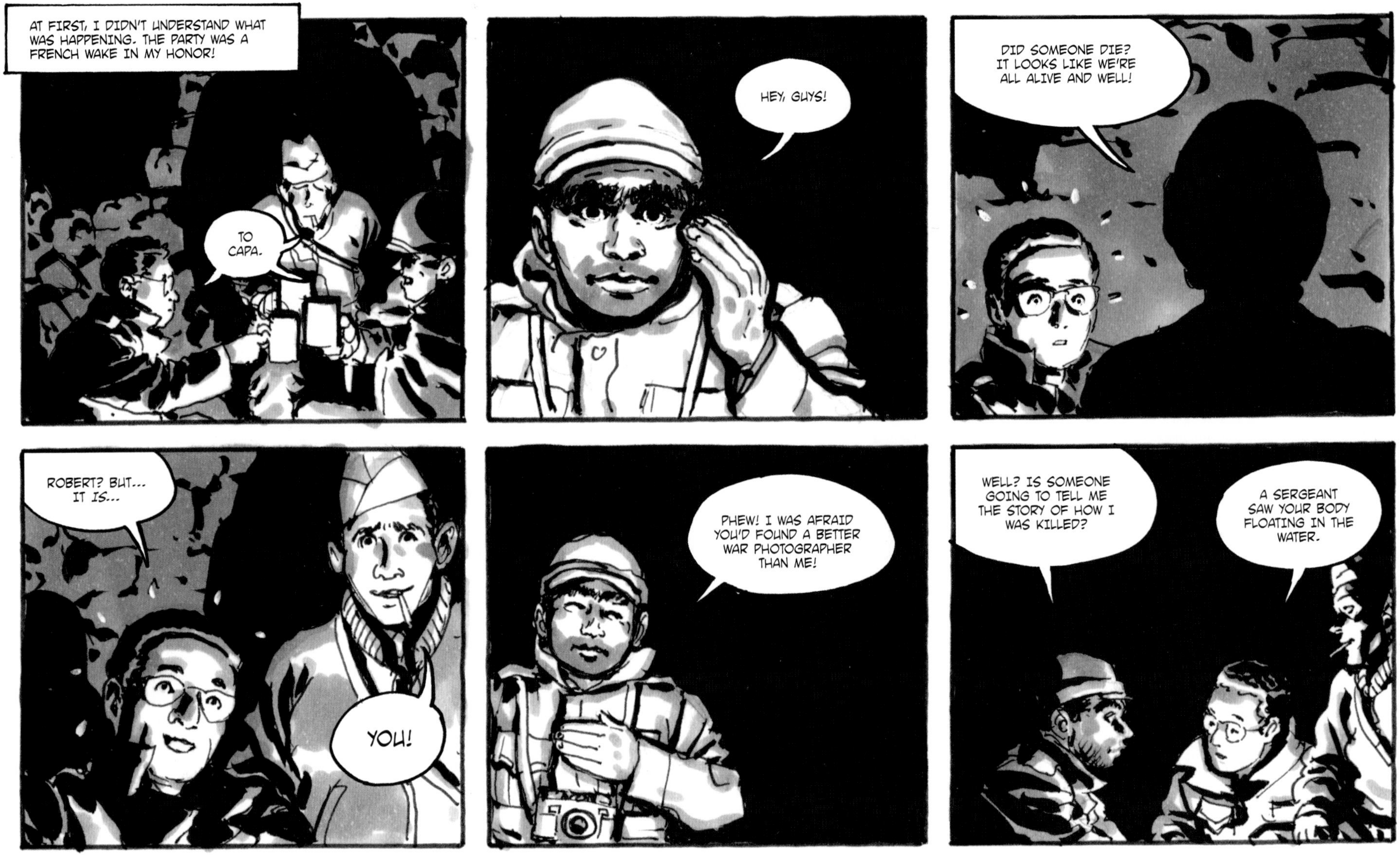
AT FIRST, I DIDN'T UNDERSTAND WHAT WAS HAPPENING. THE PARTY WAS A FRENCH WAKE IN MY HONOR!
TO CAPA.
HEY, GUYS!
DID SOMEONE DIE? IT LOOKS LIKE WE'RE ALL ALIVE AND WELL!
ROBERT? BUT... IT IS...
YOU!
PHEW! I WAS AFRAID YOU'D FOUND A BETTER WAR PHOTOGRAPHER THAN ME!
WELL? IS SOMEONE GOING TO TELL ME THE STORY OF HOW I WAS KILLED?
A SERGEANT SAW YOUR BODY FLOATING IN THE WATER.

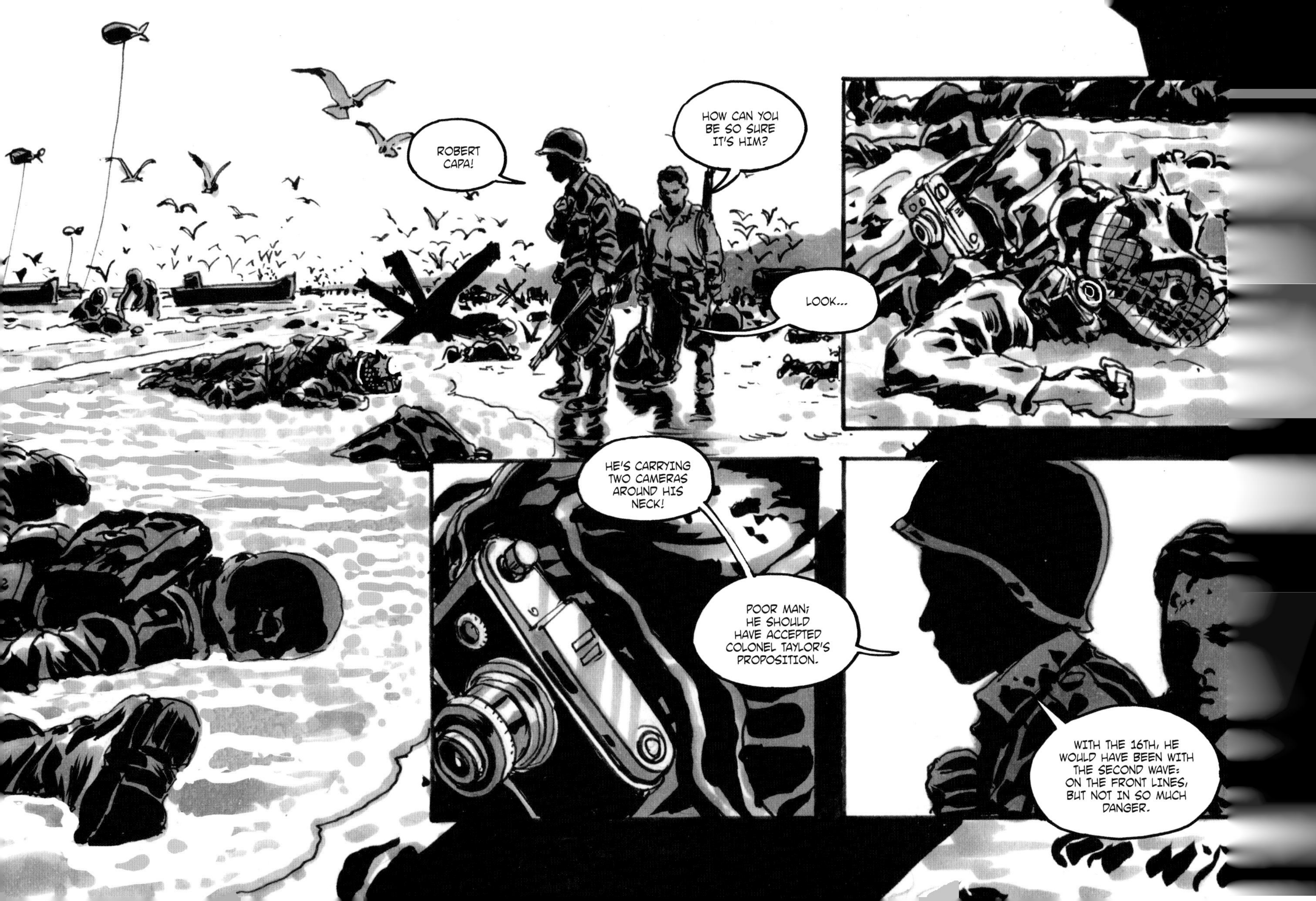
ROBERT CAPA!
HOW CAN YOU BE SO SURE IT'S HIM?
LOOK...
HE'S CARRYING TWO CAMERAS AROUND HIS NECK!
POOR MAN; HE SHOULD HAVE ACCEPTED COLONEL TAYLOR'S PROPOSITION.
WITH THE 16TH, HE WOULD HAVE BEEN WITH THE SECOND WAVE: ON THE FRONT LINES, BUT NOT IN SO MUCH DANGER.

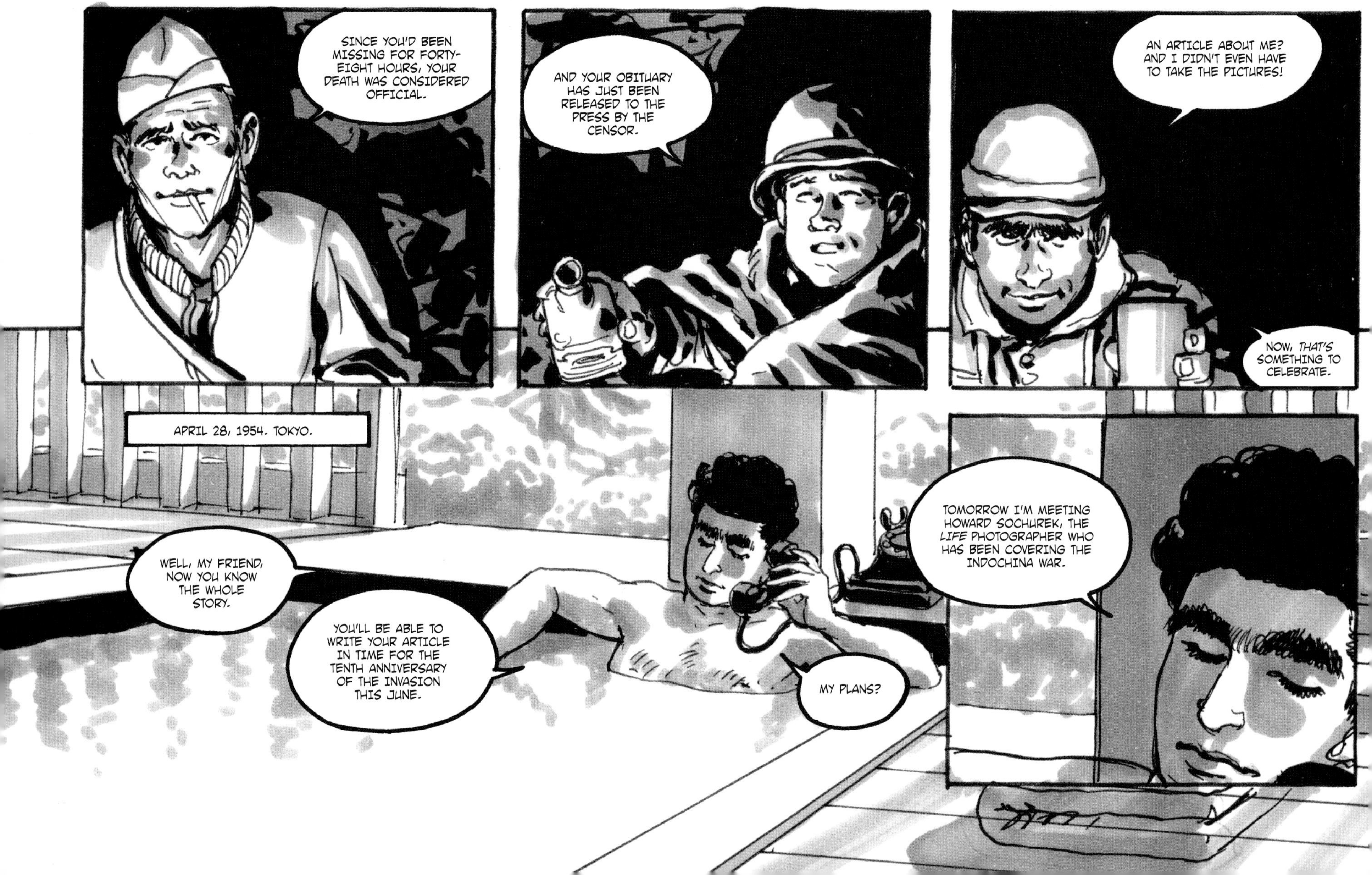
SINCE YOU'D BEEN MISSING FOR FORTY-EIGHT HOURS, YOUR DEATH WAS CONSIDERED OFFICIAL.
AND YOUR OBITUARY HAS JUST BEEN RELEASED TO THE PRESS BY THE CENSOR.
AN ARTICLE ABOUT ME? AND I DIDN'T EVEN HAVE TO TAKE THE PICTURES!
NOW, *THAT'S* SOMETHING TO CELEBRATE.
APRIL 28, 1954. TOKYO.
WELL, MY FRIEND, NOW YOU KNOW THE WHOLE STORY.
YOU'LL BE ABLE TO WRITE YOUR ARTICLE IN TIME FOR THE TENTH ANNIVERSARY OF THE INVASION THIS JUNE.
MY PLANS?
TOMORROW I'M MEETING HOWARD SOCHUREK, THE *LIFE* PHOTOGRAPHER WHO HAS BEEN COVERING THE INDOCHINA WAR.

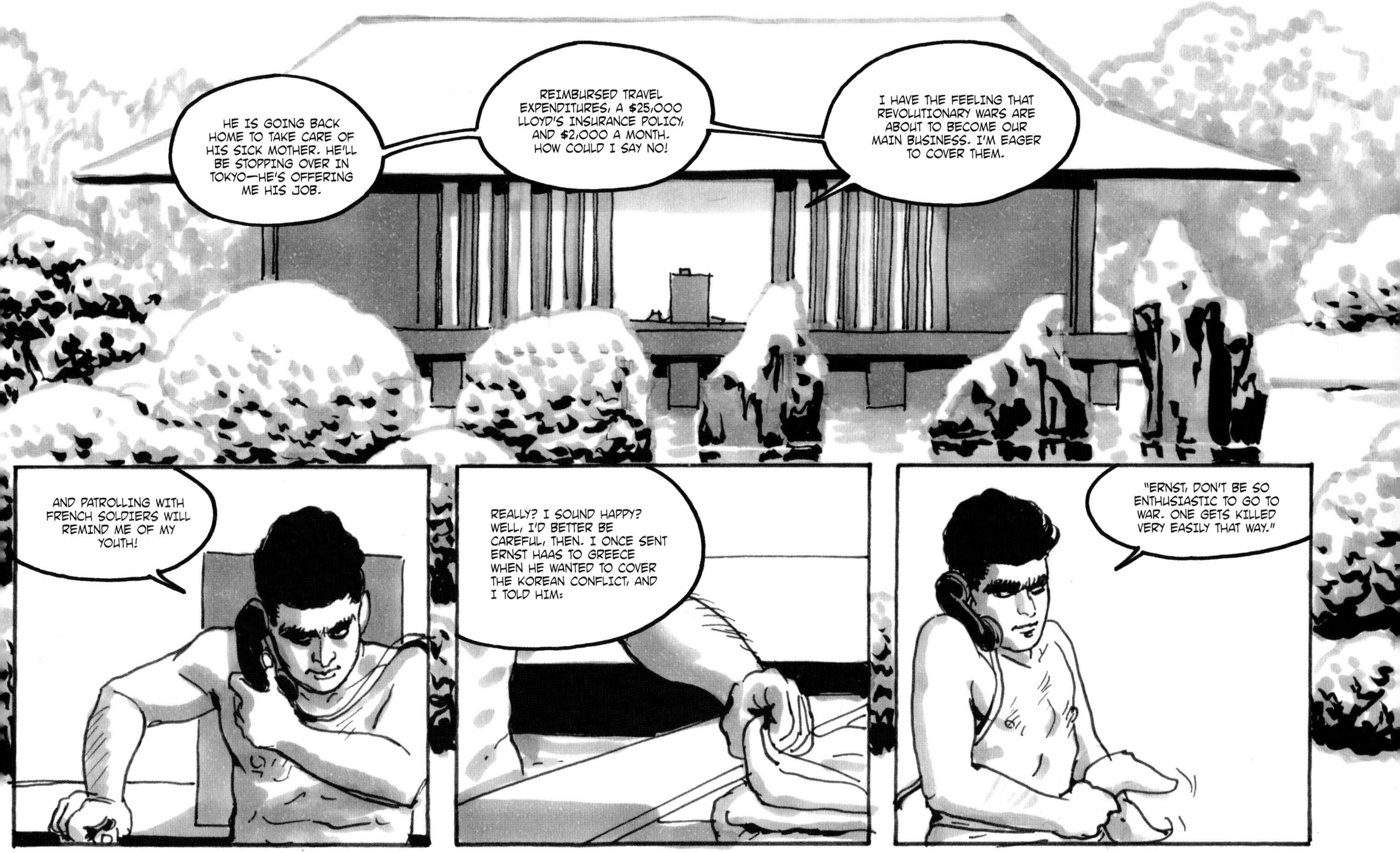
HE IS GOING BACK HOME TO TAKE CARE OF HIS SICK MOTHER. HE'LL BE STOPPING OVER IN TOKYO—HE'S OFFERING ME HIS JOB.
REIMBURSED TRAVEL EXPENDITURES, A $25,000 LLOYD'S INSURANCE POLICY, AND $2,000 A MONTH. HOW COULD I SAY NO!
I HAVE THE FEELING THAT REVOLUTIONARY WARS ARE ABOUT TO BECOME OUR MAIN BUSINESS. I'M EAGER TO COVER THEM.
AND PATROLLING WITH FRENCH SOLDIERS WILL REMIND ME OF MY YOUTH!
REALLY? I SOUND HAPPY? WELL, I'D BETTER BE CAREFUL, THEN. I ONCE SENT ERNST HAAS TO GREECE WHEN HE WANTED TO COVER THE KOREAN CONFLICT, AND I TOLD HIM:
"ERNST, DON'T BE SO ENTHUSIASTIC TO GO TO WAR. ONE GETS KILLED VERY EASILY THAT WAY."

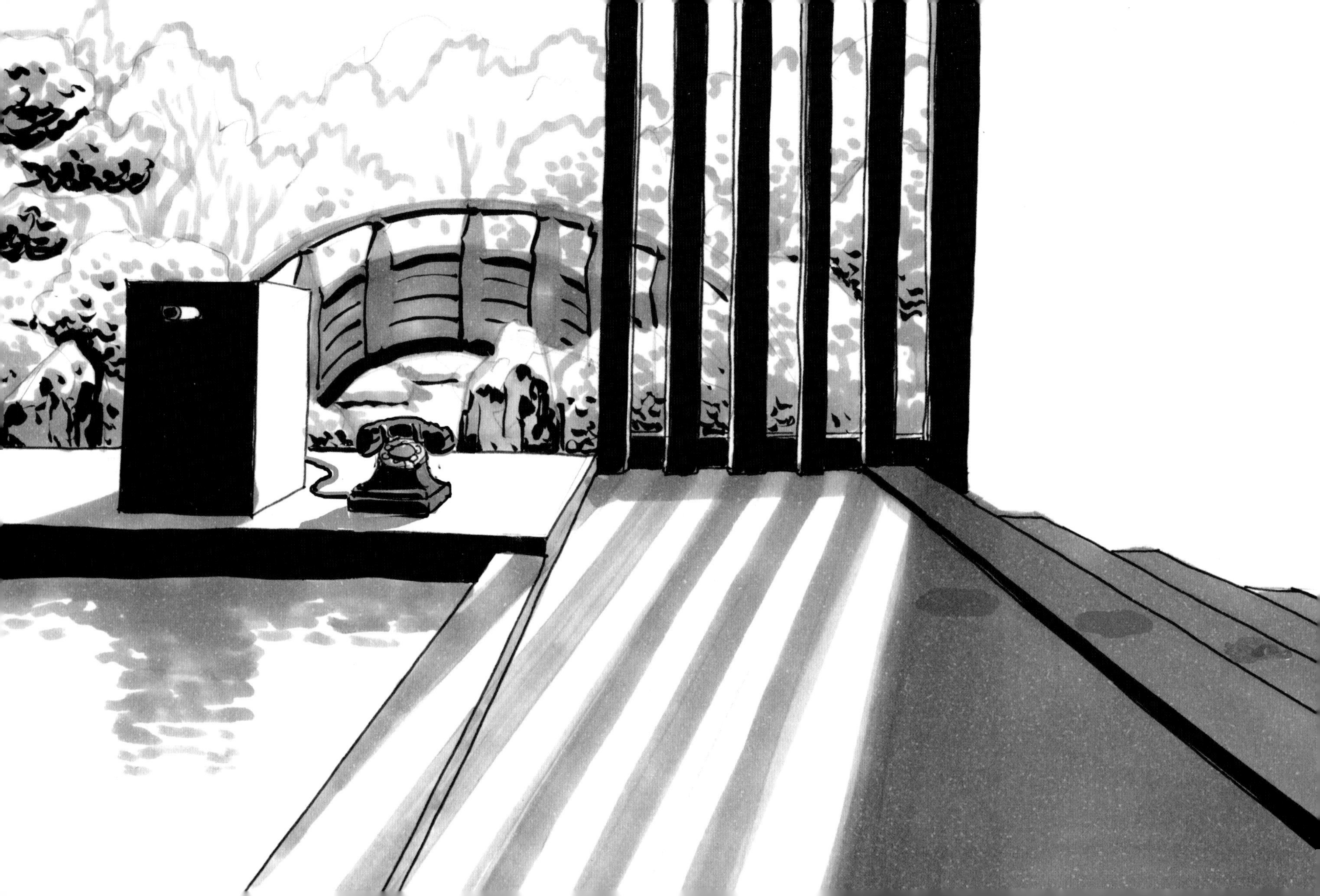

PRESS RELEASE ON MAY 28, 1954:
ON MAY 25, AT 3:10 PM IN THE SOUTH OF HANOI—
AMERICAN WAR PHOTOGRAPHER ROBERT CAPA STEPPED ON A LAND
MINE WHILE REPORTING ON RICE HARVESTING IN THE DELTA.

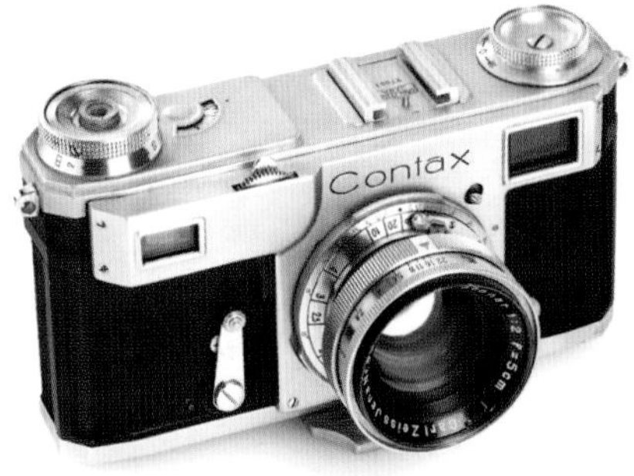
Contax

In 1937, Robert Capa adopted the Contax II, manufactured by the German company Zeiss Ikon in Dresden. He would remain faithful to the brand, preferring its viewfinder and range finder to Leica's.

Faces in the Surf

These are the only images in the world that bear witness to the first wave of the Omaha Beach landing on June 6, 1944. Just ten photos survived a drying accident in the Time-Life darkroom in London. Now, seventy years later, only nine of the original negatives remain; one was lost years ago.

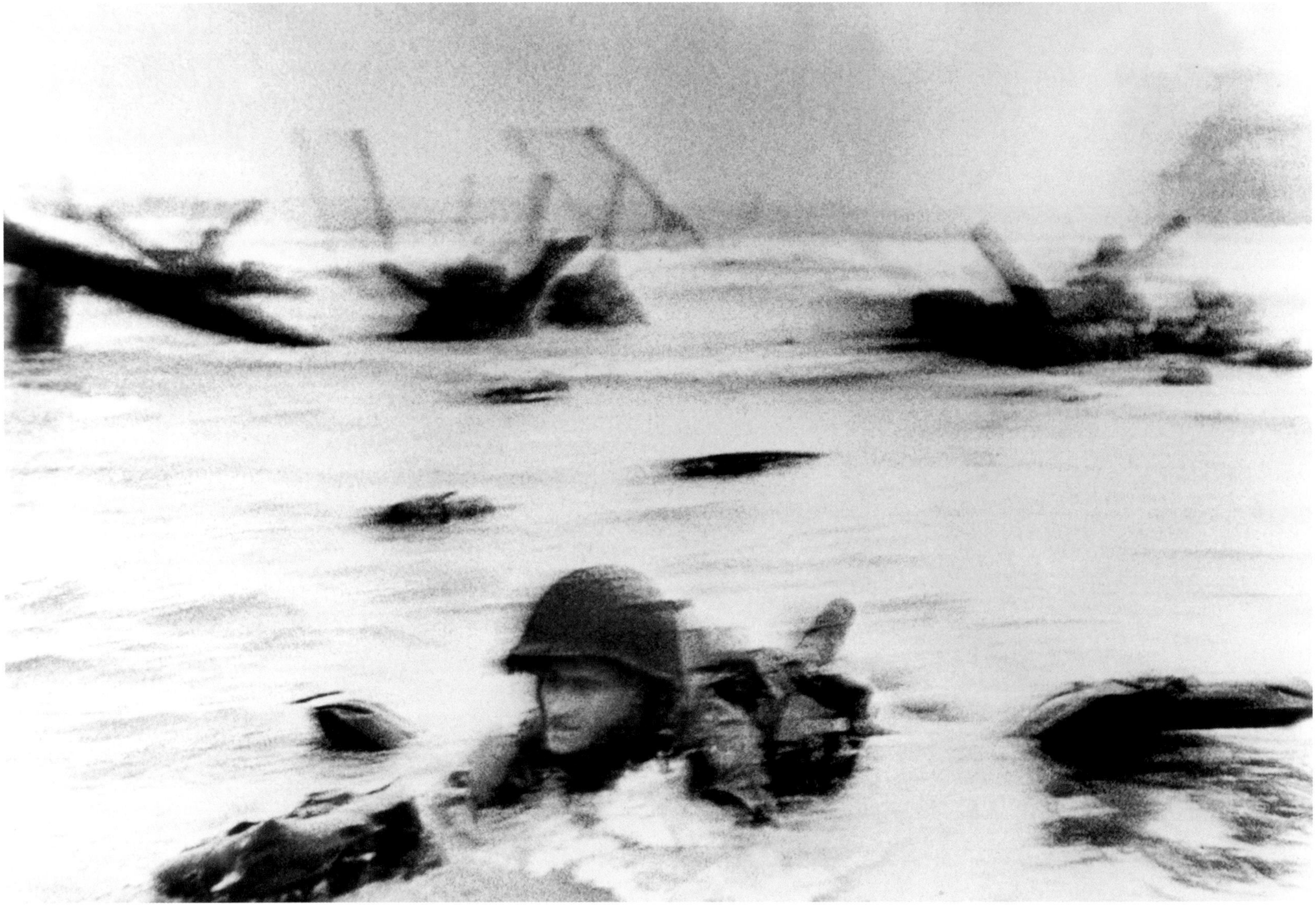

Huston S. Riley became known as *The Face in the Surf* in this iconic image.

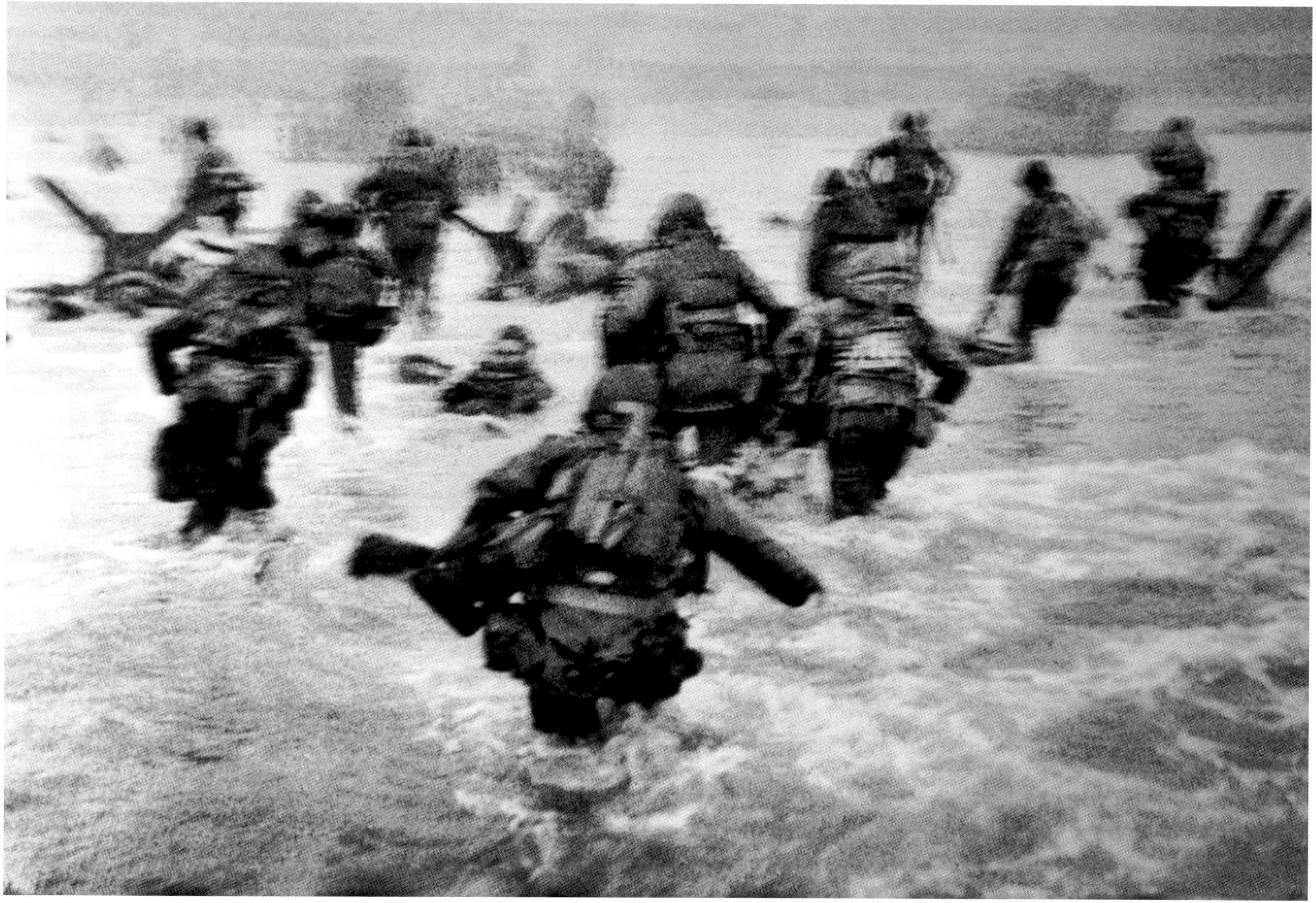

Company E from the “Big Red One” (1st Infantry Division of the US Army) leaving the landing craft.

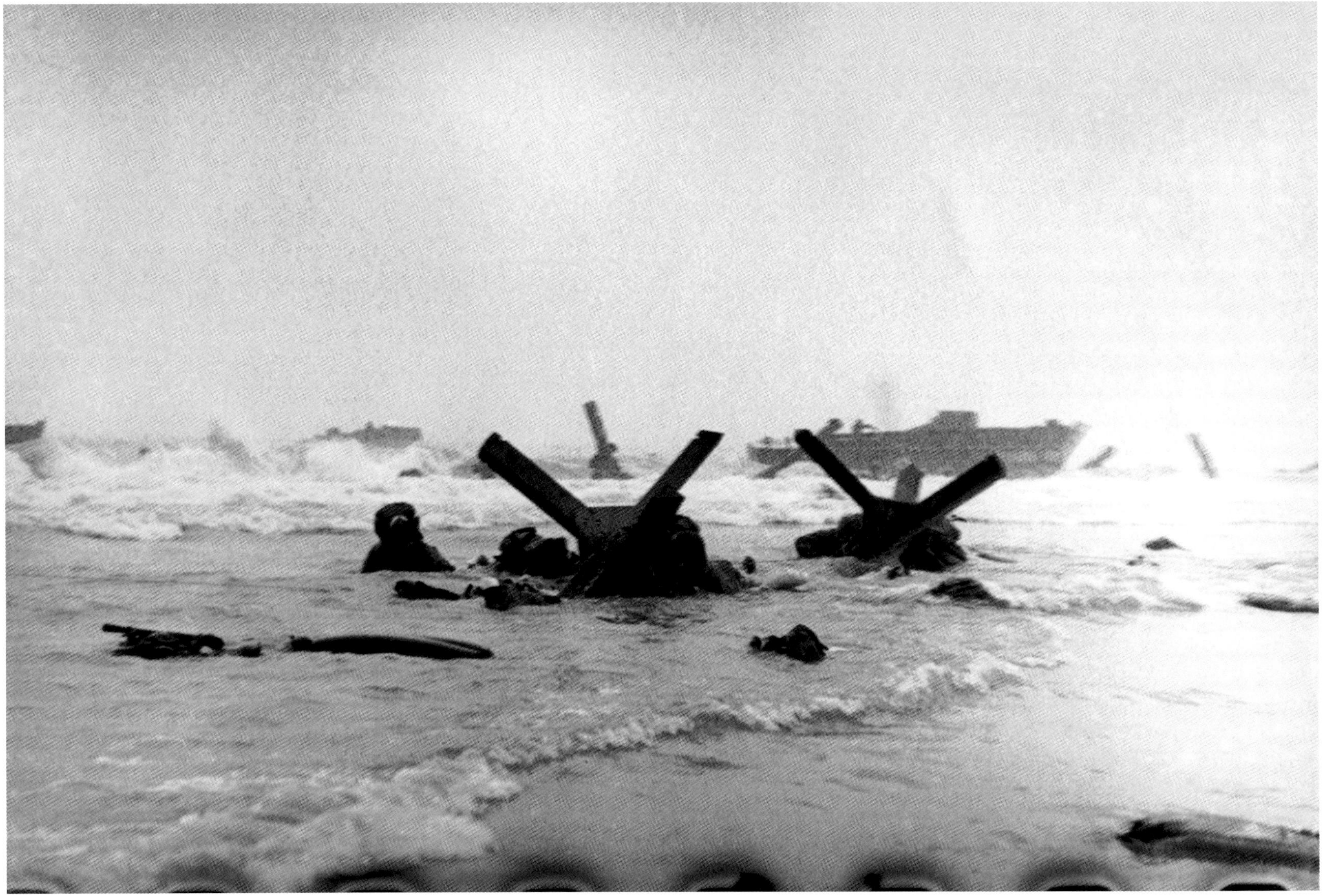

An Army engineer behind “Czech hedgehogs,” German antitank obstacles.

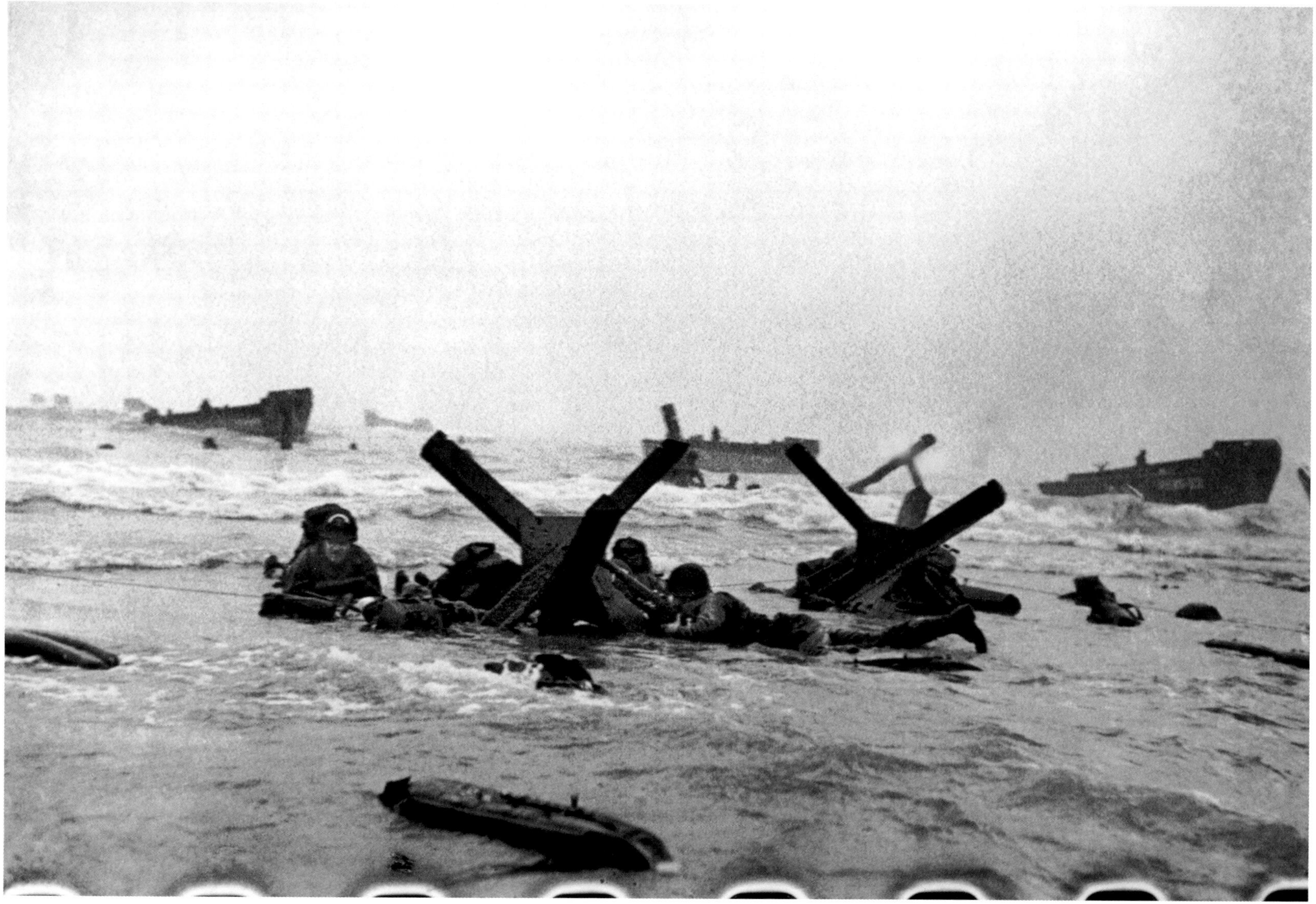

Robert Capa gets closer to his subject, exposing his back to fire from the dunes.

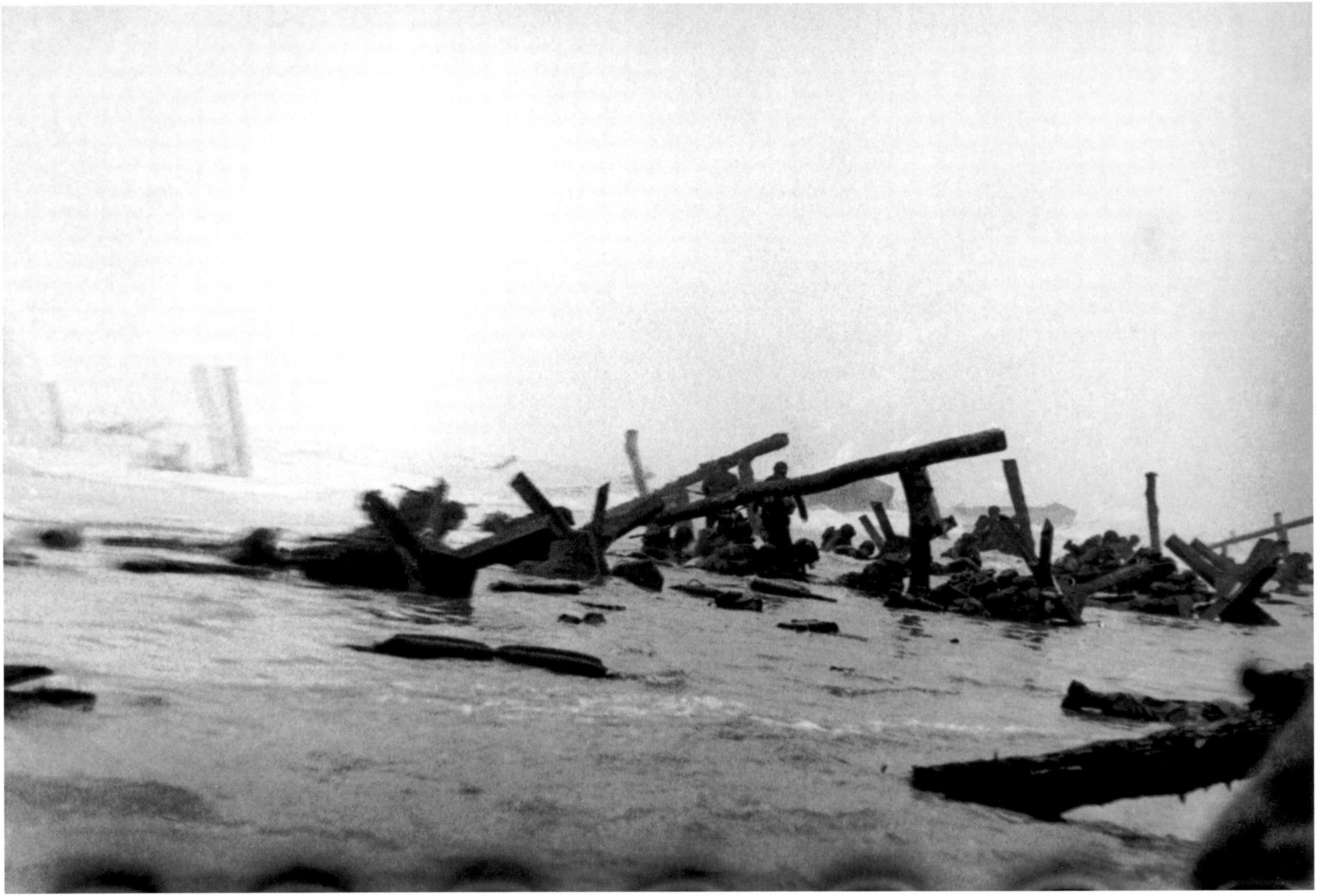

German fire keeps soldiers from getting out of the water and onto the beach.

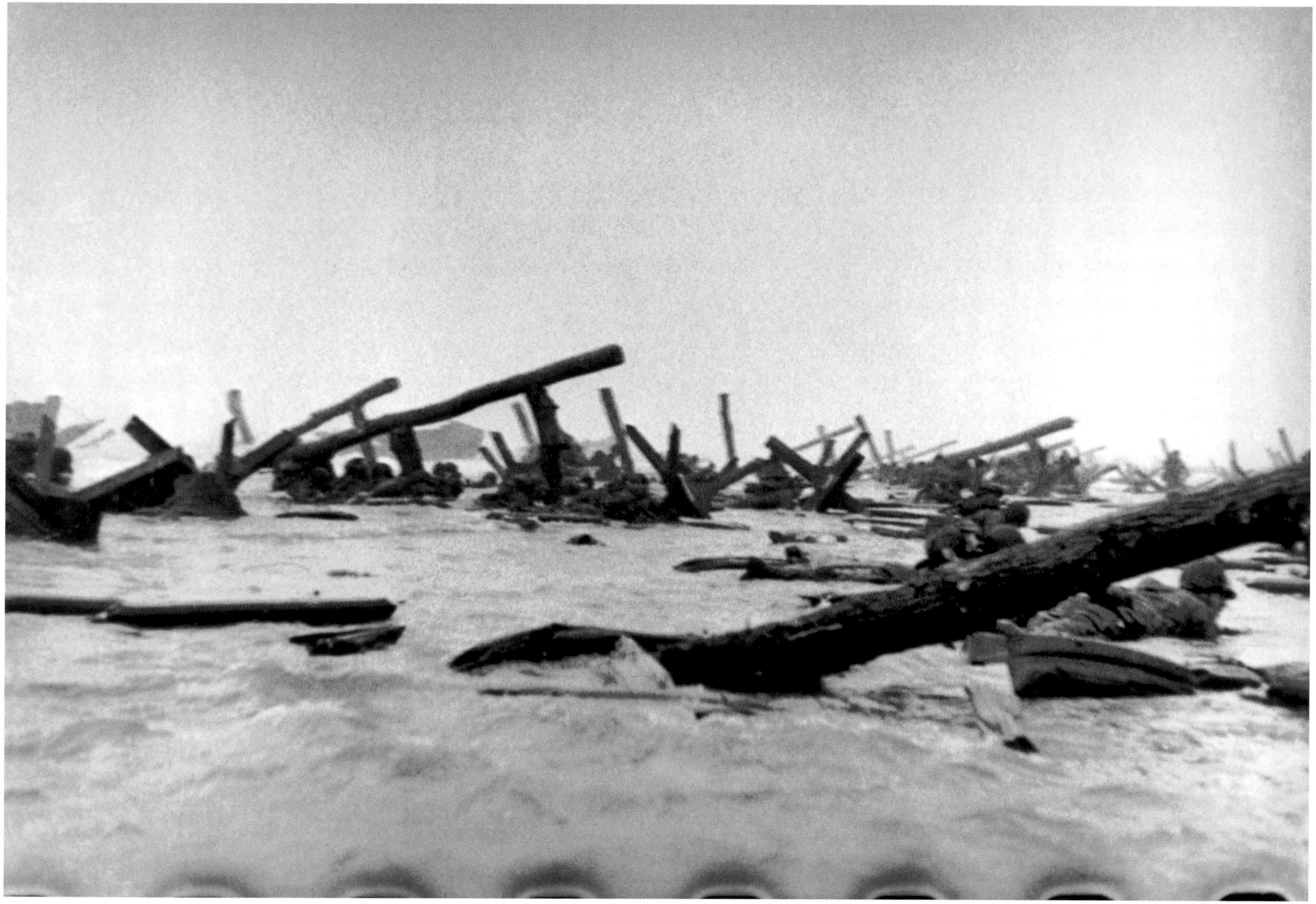

American soldiers take cover behind the *Rommelspargel* ("Rommel's asparagus"), an anti-landing craft defense.

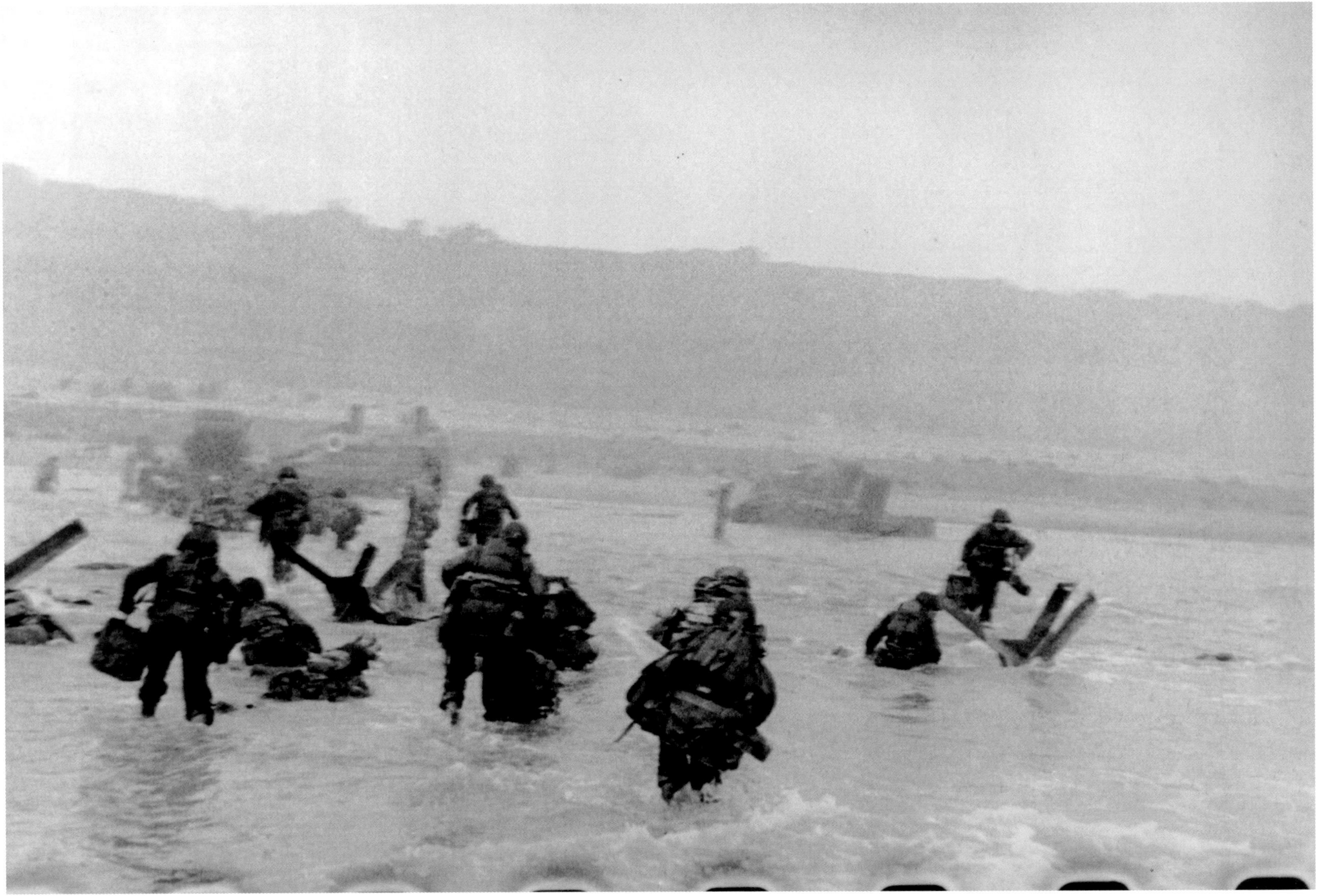

Soaking wet and carrying heavy packs, the soldiers advance to the beach.

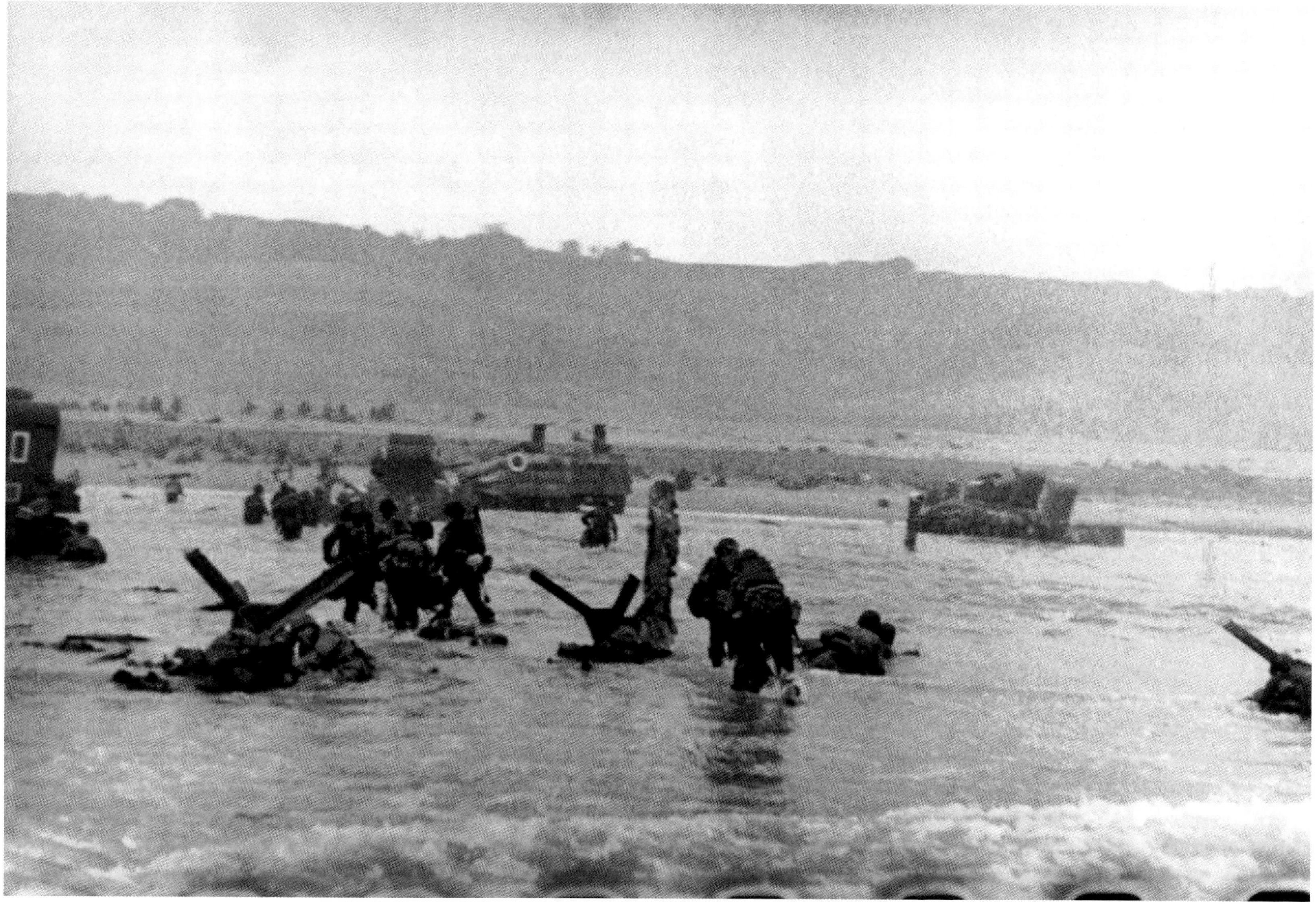

Intense German fire from atop the dunes—an imposing height, seen from the sea. The few amphibious tanks, meant to break through the lines, have already broken down.

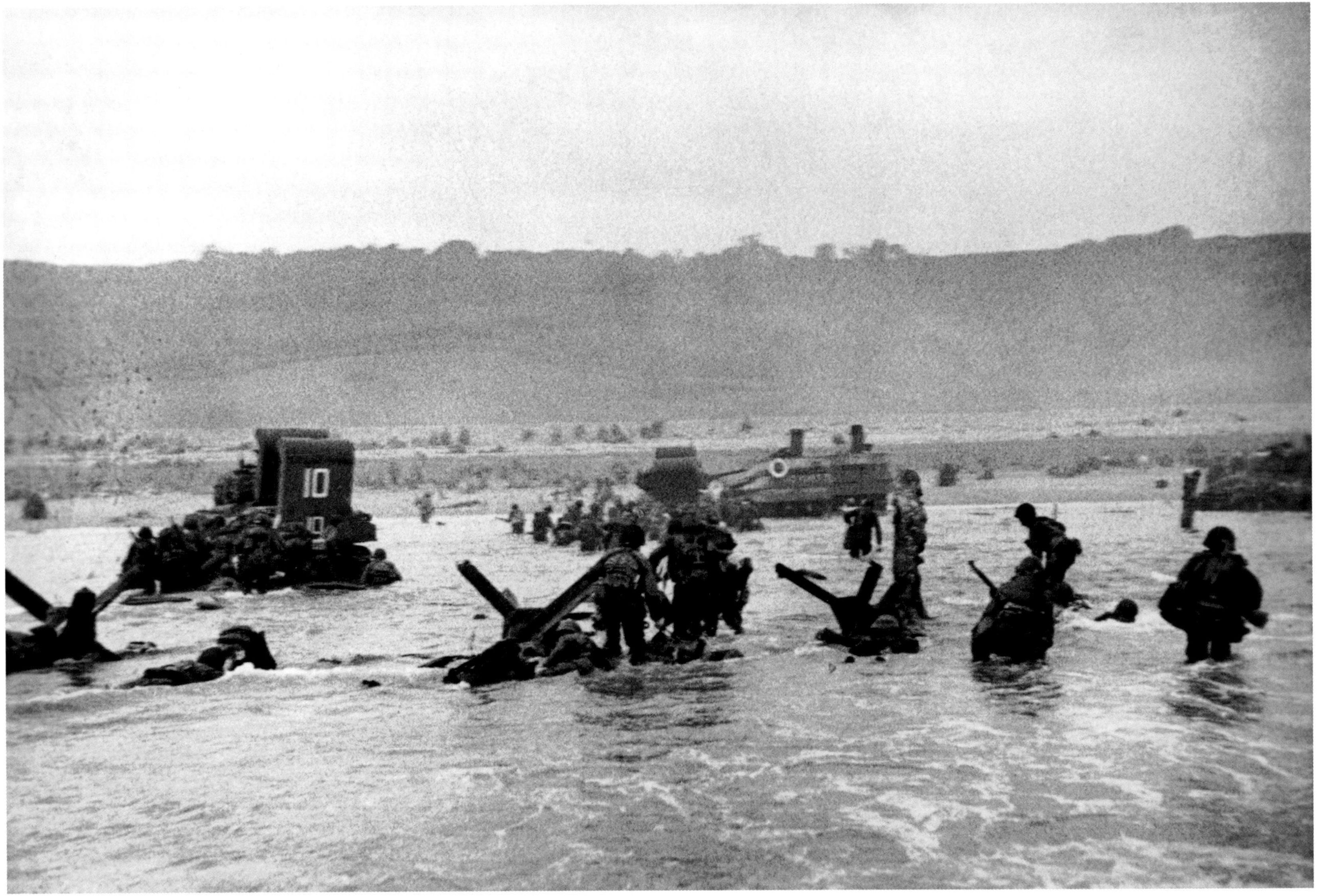

Only amphibious tank No. 10 still seems to be moving. The soldiers take cover behind its armor plating.

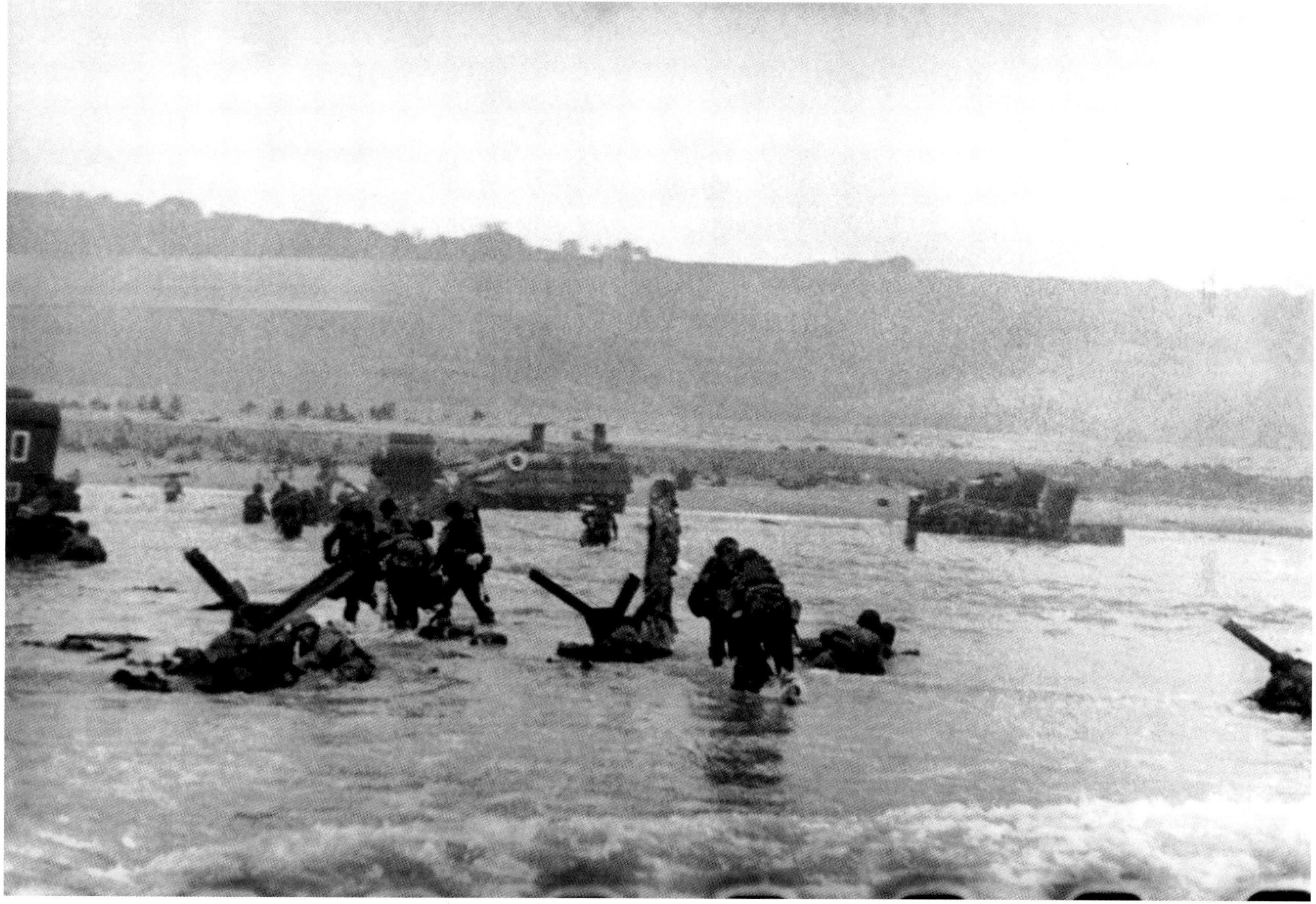

The dune in the background, six miles long, is part of Saint-Laurent-sur-Mer, one of three villages in the Calvados department along Omaha Beach.

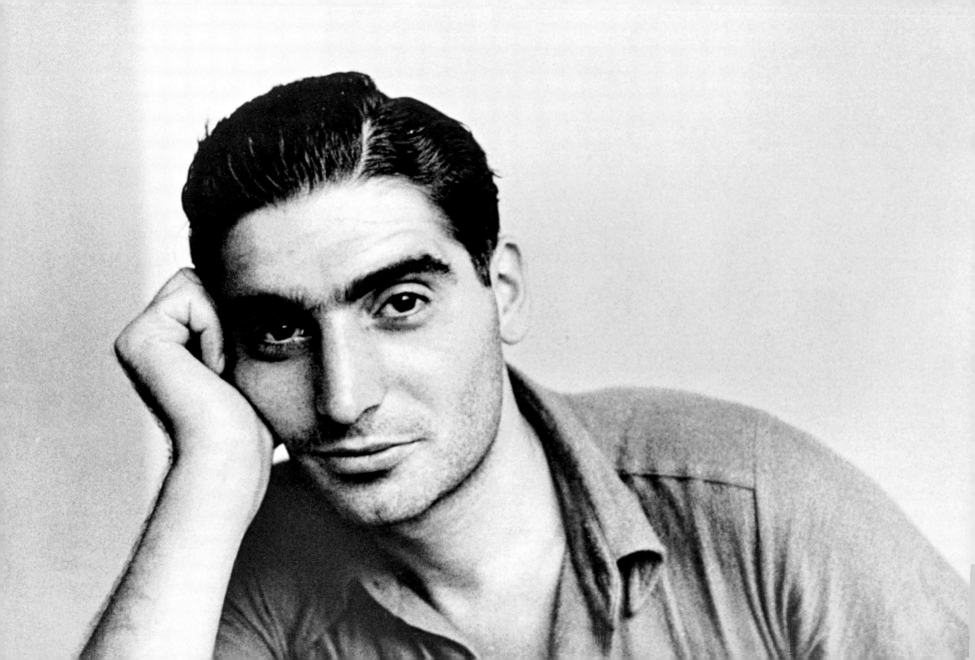

The man who invented himself

American soldiers during the "Battle of the Hedgerows," amid hedged farmland along the English Channel. Normandy. July 1944.
OPPOSITE André Friedmann, a.k.a. Robert Capa, in Paris. Fall 1935.

Roberta Capa is without a doubt one of the fathers of photojournalism. His style of always being at the heart of the action, always close to his subjects; how he could build and tell a story in pictures, for the newly popular magazine press; how a few of his famous images are slightly out of focus, and still the framing is ever meaningful—it has made him an internationally recognized master and pioneer.

Capa was one of the "concerned photographers": Politically engaged with his times, he went on to cover five wars. To bear witness, do research, retain control of his negatives and his own legend, provide work for an independent cooperative of photographers by generously distributing both ideas and assignments—these were the goals of his brief professional life. Blown up by a land mine at the age of forty in Indochina after

Celebrating the liberation of Cherbourg. June 28, 1944.

a meteoric twenty-two year career, he bequeathed to humanity 70,000 images still cherished some sixty years after his death.

In 2013, when Paris Photo was opening its doors to the public, several friends of Bob's gathered at his last Parisian home, the Hôtel Lancaster on rue de Berri. It was the hundredth anniversary of his birth. In this palace, his generous Swiss patron Emile Wolf had granted him a maid's garret. Capa left behind a few tailored suits and shirts, camera cases and lenses, some Simenon books in English, and many debts.

Capa was a gambler, and his passions for horse racing and poker didn't always bring him luck—except on a certain June 6, 1944: "The war correspondent has his stake—his life—in his own hands, and he can put it on this horse or that horse, or he can put it back in his pocket at the very last minute. I am a gambler. I decided to go in with Company E in the first wave," Capa wrote in his memoir, *Slightly Out of Focus*, published in the spring of 1947.

Endre, Robert, and Bob

There were three distinct periods in Capa's short life, and the names Endre, Robert, and Bob define who he was in each of them. Born in 1913 in a rapidly collapsing Hungarian empire, Endre Ernö Friedmann was the eldest son of a family of tailors of Jewish descent from Budapest. As a student, he frequented artistic circles. He liked girls, books, and the great outdoors.

When faced with the authoritarian regime of Admiral Horthy's regency during his high school years, he campaigned for civil liberties and fought against dictatorship. After being arrested during a demonstration, he decided to leave the country. In 1931, he left for Berlin. As a journalism student at the German Academy for Politics, he supported himself by working as a darkroom technician for the Dephot agency, run at the time by fellow countryman Simon Guttmann. In Copenhagen, Capa covered one of Trotsky's rare European rallies with his Leica (the basic model with a fixed lens), producing portraits that became instant classics.

In September 1933, having fled Nazi Germany, Endre became André and continued his exile in the "City of Light," where he would soon celebrate his twentieth birthday. Lacking means but never without his Leica, he would try to get by in Paris. His networks, new friends, and the people he met in Montparnasse came to his rescue. David "Chim" Seymour, Henri Cartier-

Ruins of a church in the Saint-Lô region of Normandy. July 1944.

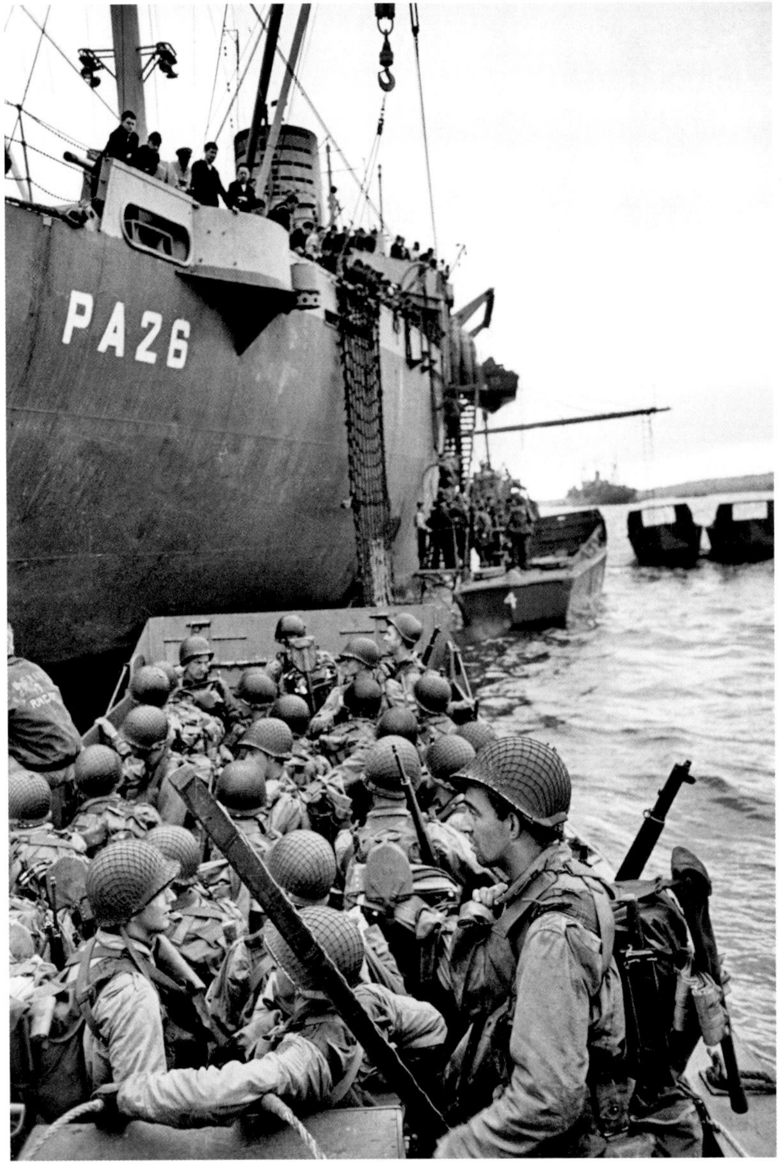
PA26

Bresson, Capa's companion Gerta Pohorylle, and also Louis Aragon, Paul Nizan, Lucien Vogel (founder of *Vu* magazine), and even Maria Eisner, who ran the Alliance Photo agency, would all contribute to launching his career. Friedmann was openly involved with progressive Leftist circles, travelers of the French Communist Party, and above all, fellow anti-fascist exiles.

In 1934, no doubt under Gerta's influence (she had renamed herself Gerda Taro), André became Robert Capa—not just any pseudonym, but one that sounded American. In short, André donned, like a new suit, the persona of a man he'd invented from scratch.

Starting in 1936 with the publication of Capa's famous photograph from Andalusia, *The Falling Soldier*, Taro and Capa's signatures could be found in the most prominent news magazines of the day. In fewer than four years, the man who'd shown up penniless in Paris with nothing but a suitcase to his name would become, in the words of London's *Picture Post*, "the greatest war photographer in the world." But Gerda Taro's accidental death in July 1937, during the Battle of Brunete in Spain, would plunge him into the depths of despair.

American troops leaving for France.
Port of Weymouth, England. June 4, 1944.

Gaining Professional Independence

When the Third Reich's troops invaded Paris in June 1940, Capa's world was turned upside down. Like so many other admirers of France—a bastion of freedom—he had never believed the country would fall. At the time, he was in Mexico, working for *Life* magazine. In September 1939, Capa had abruptly left Paris and his studio at 37, rue Froidevaux, Montparnasse, for New York, where his mother Julia and his brother Cornell had been living in exile since 1934. Capa also had a good number of American friends—Ernest Hemingway among them, whom he'd met at the Hotel Florida in Madrid and grown close to during the Spanish Civil War. It was said that Capa greatly improved his English in Hemingway's company.

The stateless Friedmann would become Bob Capa, an American citizen, in 1946.

His coverage of World War II, which earned him the Presidential Medal of Freedom in 1947, sealed his reputation. He was finally able to fulfill an old dream: to gain professional independence by creating a photographers' cooperative—Magnum Photos. At the MoMA restaurant in New York, a few longtime friends gathered over drinks (champagne, no doubt): David

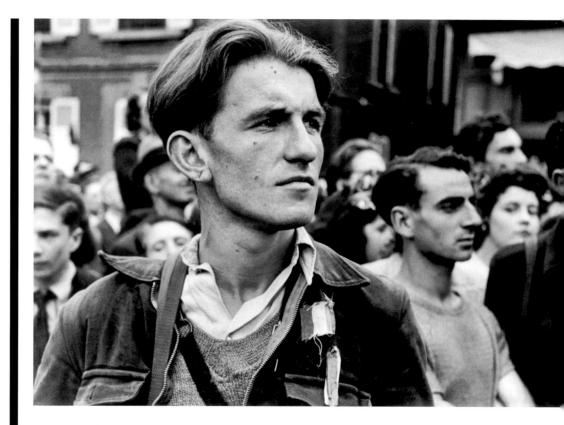

A young Resistance fighter listening to General de Gaulle's speech at Chartres on the day the town was liberated. August 23, 1944.

A spot known as "Le Riquet" on Omaha Beach. June 1944.

OVERLEAF Norman fishermen gazing at the bodies of dead soldiers. Omaha Beach. June 8, 1944.

ferred another quote—"It's not always easy to stand aside and be unable to do anything except record the sufferings around one."

One day in Paris, Capa gave Magnum's young recruits the following advice: "Love the people you photograph. They'll always give it back to you."

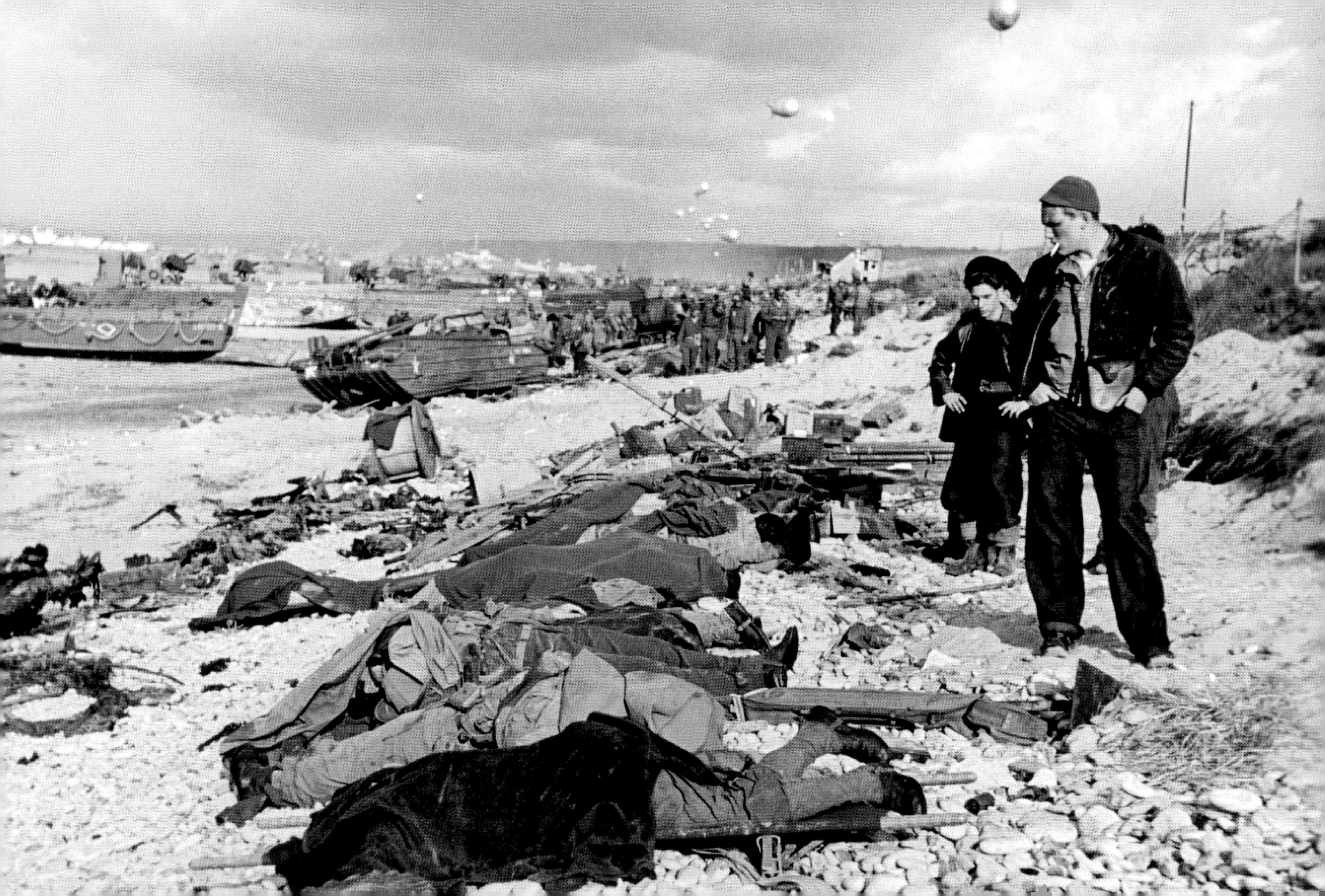

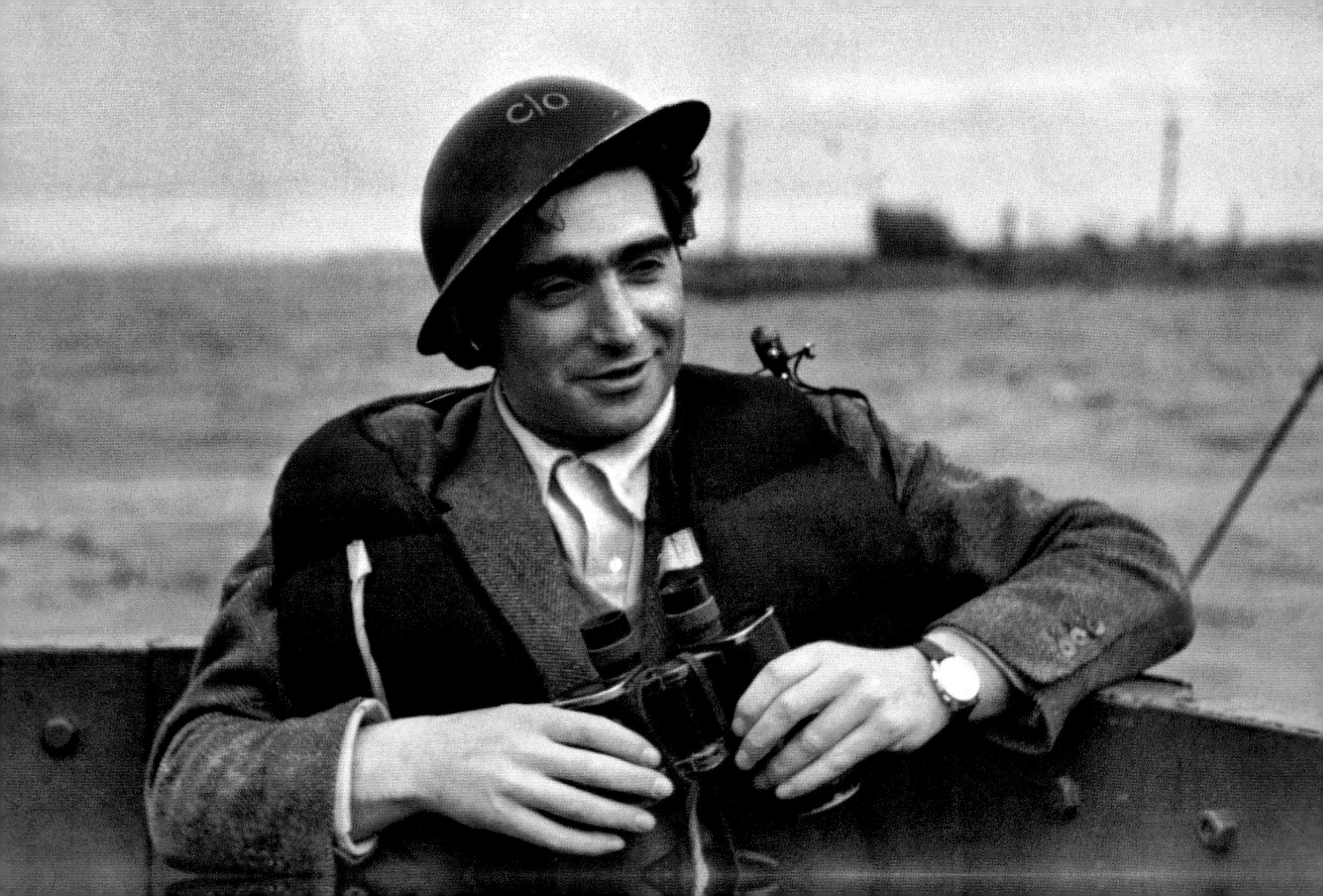
C/O

The eye of June 6, 1944

American troops taking a landing craft to D-Day transport ship, Weymouth, England, June 4, 1944.
OPPOSITE Robert Capa reporting for *Collier's* magazine, aboard a convoy of Liberty Ships on the Atlantic. These vessels, supporting the war in Britain, were often attacked by German U-boats.

Dawn on Tuesday, June 6, 1944, found no fewer than thirteen war correspondents in the ranks of the US First Army soldiers assigned to Normandy's Omaha sector. And they weren't just any correspondents—the cream of the journalistic crop had started reporting for duty at 0630 hours. All the major American newspapers had their special dispatches (reporting from "somewhere in France"—just where was top secret): the *New York Herald Tribune*, *Chicago Tribune*, *Los Angeles Times*, and many others. Representing radio was the famous John MacVane of NBC, who set foot on land at Saint-Laurent-sur-Mer without his transmitter. It wouldn't reach him until the next day. There would be words—written and spoken—but no pictures. At least, not from the beach.

Medical barge off Omaha Beach, taking in the wounded from the landing. June 6, 1944.

Of these US war correspondents, one and one alone would achieve the impossible that day: Robert Capa, who would go down in history as the eye of June 6, 1944. Capa was thirty at the time, with two wars (Spain and China) under his belt, as well as a record of brilliant work in North Africa, Great Britain, Sicily, and Italy at decisive turning points of World War II. On top of all that, he knew, inside and out, the country in which he was about to land with the first wave.

No Photos of Dead Soldiers!

Capa had lived in France, his second home, from 1933 to 1939, and had mastered the language, just as he had English. On D-day, he was still a staff photographer for *Life* magazine but also a member of the "Press Photographers, Western Front" pool, which John Godfrey Morris in London—photo editor for Time-Life Bureau—had been put in charge of by Supreme Headquarters Allied Expeditionary Force (SHAEF), headed by General Dwight D. Eisenhower in Europe.

In short, Capa had an enormous responsibility on his shoulders. The army would make his pictures available for free to press services all over the world (after censorship, of course: no photos of dead soldiers on the beach were allowed). *Life* magazine was able to get an accredited photographer in the first wave, and naturally, the job was entrusted to a photographer of great renown.

Of the four photographers the US Army picked for the June 6 landing, two were from *Life* magazine, and two were veterans. Capa was assigned to the Omaha Beach sector, and Bob Landry (one of the only professional photographers present during the attack on Pearl Harbor on December 7, 1941) to the Utah Beach sector. Landry was unlucky. When his pictures were shipped across the Channel to England that day, all his rolls of film disappeared.

Dubbed "Overlord," the largest combined military operation of all time consisted of 11,590 aircraft, 3,500 gliders, and 4,308 vessels, and resulted in 150,000 men landing in France. It took years of preparation and unprecedented military planning. Since 1942, the idea of opening a second front in Western Europe to help the Soviets had been in the works. But only after the Tehran Conference, where the three principal Allies against the Third Reich—Churchill, Roosevelt, and Stalin—were united for the first time, that the decision was made

Aboard the USS *Henrico*, off Omaha Beach: the bodies of American soldiers slain during the landing. June 6, 1944.

Port of Weymouth, England. June 4, 1944. American troops leaving for France.

at last to land in Normandy as well as the south of France. This was the famous "pincer movement" the Allied generals had devised.

330 Days of Intensive Warfare

Stalin accused his allies of scheming, of contributing to the massacre of his country and troops with their lack of an outright offensive. The demand for a second front in northwestern Europe would become a leitmotif of Soviet propaganda. It became essential to show Moscow, with pictures, that the Normandy landing had indeed happened, that considerable relief efforts were underway, and that the road to Berlin was open at last.

As a reminder: Counting from D-day on, it took the Allied forces—including General Leclerc's French 2nd Armored Division—one hundred days to liberate Paris (three times longer than foreseen in the Overlord plans) and two hundred days after that to reach Berlin. Once the success of Overlord was certain, the (partial) liberation of Europe still required ten straight months of intensive warfare.

And before any of that, the infamous "Fortress Europe" had to be breached, surrounded by what was commonly known as the "Atlantic Wall," fortifications extending along the coast of the English Channel. Depicted as unbreakable in Nazi propaganda, but well known to be weak between the Seine estuary and Cherbourg, its solidity seemed to be a source of great worry for the man in charge—Field Marshall Rommel—if his reports are any indication. The Allies hoped to exploit these weaknesses along the fifty miles of Norman coast stretching between the Orne and Vire estuaries. Five landing sectors were designated by code names: Utah and Omaha for the American side; Gold, Juno, and Sword for the Canadians.

"Bloody Omaha" would earn its terrible nickname on the evening of June 6. Half the D-day losses occurred on these six miles of sand. More than 4,000 men died. By comparison, losses were limited to 200 men at Utah Beach, 600 at Sword, and 1,000 at Juno.

The tragedy of Omaha Beach is often blamed on bad weather conditions. Six-foot waves, Force 4 winds, and strong coastal currents threw the painstakingly laid plans into chaos. The shallow water beached landing craft several hundred yards from shore, leaving GIs

Omaha Beach.

German POWs taken by Americans. Omaha Beach. June 1944.

open to enemy fire. But in reality, the failure of Allied bombardments along the coast, as well as flaws in military intelligence, which failed to account for the presence of German reinforcements nearby, seem to be likelier causes of the disaster.

The Beachhead Strategy

This much is known: Around 8:30 AM on Tuesday, June 6, 1944 (two hours after the operation began), General Bradley, head of the US First Army, almost stopped the Omaha sector assault, as the rising losses reaching him on the radio were making it seem like, in his words, an "irreversible catastrophe." Yet the architects of the invasion had anticipated even higher losses. According to these strategists, the tactic of using sheer numbers (frighteningly called "establishing a beachhead"), with even more men in reserve, would end up winning the day, if at the cost of much bloodshed.

With a wealth of ingenuity and special effects, Steven Spielberg worked unrelentingly to reconstitute how hellish Omaha Beach must have been in the opening scene of the multiple Oscar–winning *Saving Private Ryan*. And Spielberg has stated, in most interviews about the film, that without Robert Capa's photographs, he never could have attempted a depiction of these events.

American troops leaving for France. Port of Weymouth, England. June 4, 1944.

Victims of the fighting on Omaha Beach. June 1944.

there was hardly any competition in the marketplace. And certainly not on the beach.

The other photographers, who never left the landing craft, beat Capa back to London with their film. Their images only showed the fighting from a distance, and obviously were much less striking. But their photographs had the merit of being the first ones taken off the Normandy shore, making the landing a reality for many people. They went around the world, thanks to news agencies and the shared pool of photos set up by the Army.

But through the telemetric lens of his Contax, Capa added his own eyewitness account of history in the making. It is absolutely unique, and remains irreplaceable.

For fans of raincoats and men's fashion, one small, final detail on the fate of Capa's Burberry coat can be found on page 140 of the paperback edition of his memoir (Capa, 2001): *Fifty yards ahead of me, one of our half-burnt amphibious tanks stuck out of the water and offered me my next cover. I sized up the situation. There was little future for the elegant raincoat heavy on my arm. I dropped it and made for the tank.*

And that was how a hint of civilian elegance straight from Regent Street came to be abandoned on the sand of Omaha Beach.

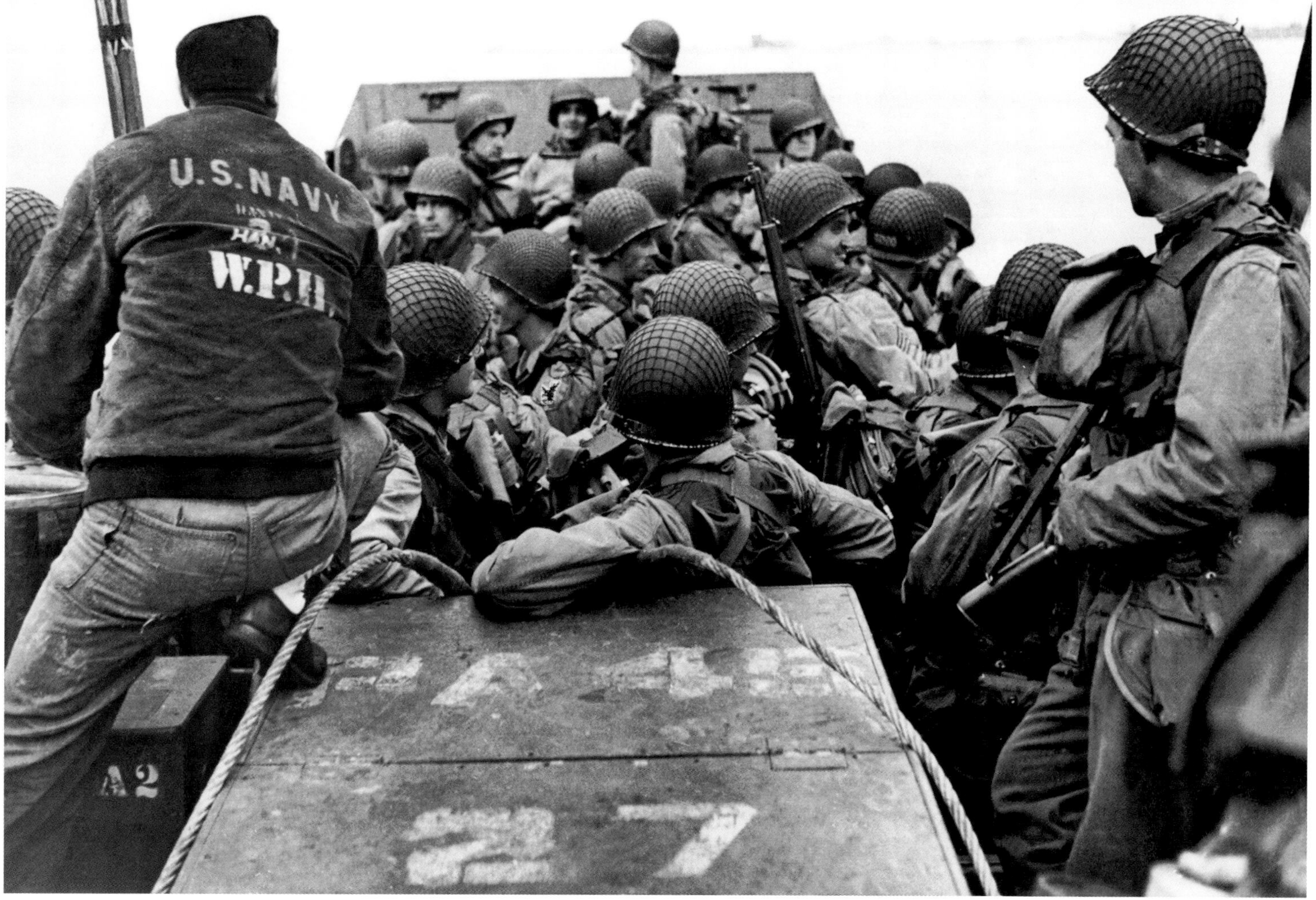
U.S.NAVY
W.P.H.
A2
27

A landing craft off Weymouth, England, heading seaward to US Navy ships waiting in the Channel. June 4, 1944.

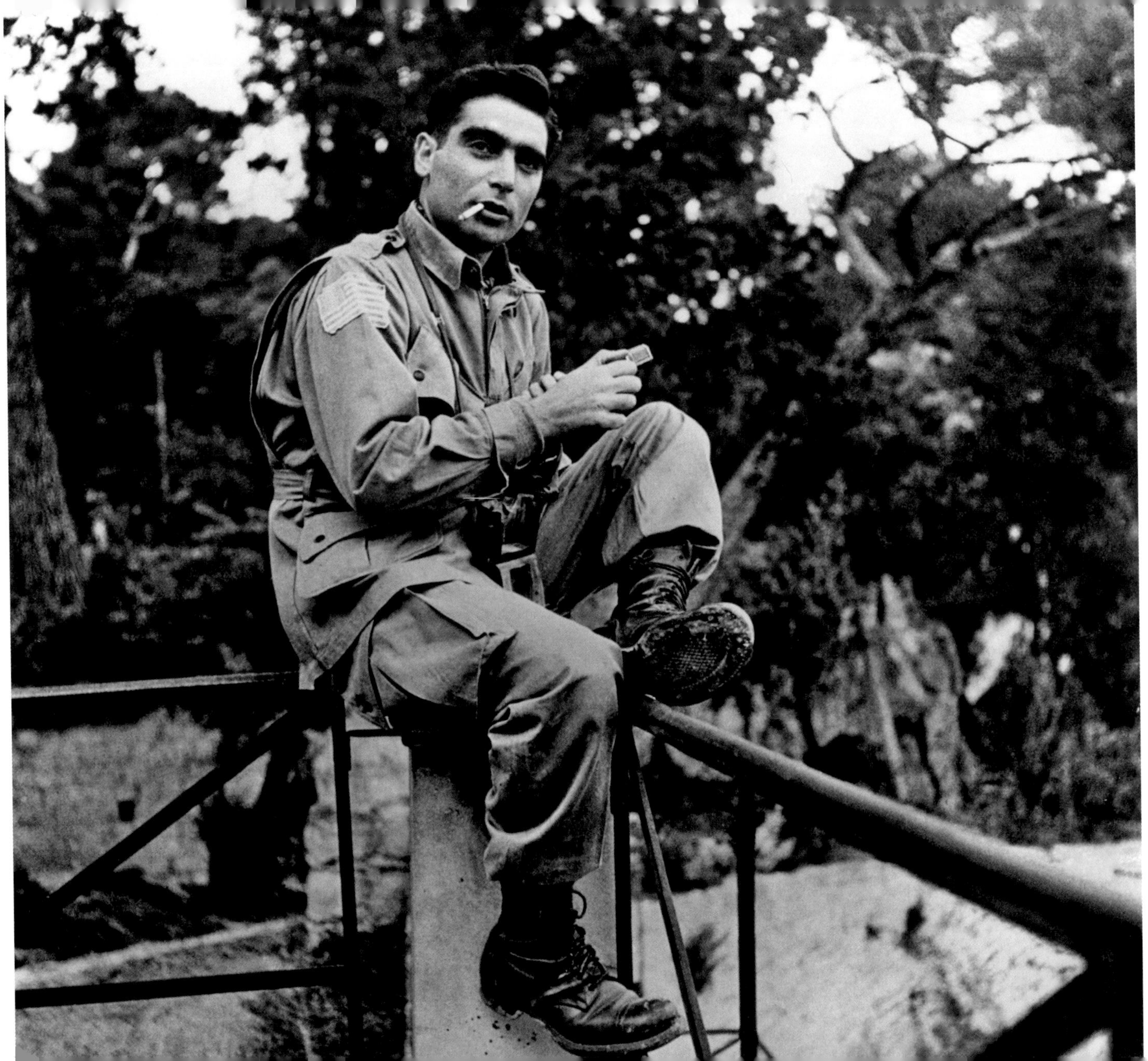

A face (lost) in the waves

American soldiers near Saint-Lô. July 26, 1944.
OPPOSITE Robert Capa during the Italian campaign, resting on the Isle of Capri. Photo by George Rodger, 1943.

As spring of 1944 drew to a close in England, bad weather conditions would upset plans the Allies had set in motion long ago.

We must look long and hard into this gap—between what was planned and what actually happened—to understand where exactly on Omaha Beach Robert Capa was on June 6, 1944.

How to find one man in a massive operation consisting of more than 133,000 soldiers on the first day alone, who were deployed over more than 4,000 landing points of varying sizes? Harder yet: trying to identify the soldier in one of Capa's famous photographs! Identifying a man lost amidst the surf, in a picture slightly out of focus, printed from a negative accidentally fogged during development, is a challenge. You'd have better luck looking for a needle in a haystack!

American soldiers during the Battle of Normandy. June–July, 1944.

Yet this was the very challenge an American academic took up in 2007. His name was Lowell L. Getz, Professor Emeritus of Animal Biology at the University of Illinois (Urbana-Champaign). An Army Reserve colonel in the Medical Corps and former member of military intelligence, this doctor of science was also involved in searching for MIAs—soldiers who have disappeared—in Vietnam and elsewhere. This gave him extensive experience with the Army's archives.

Two Hours in Total

The first thing the professor did was gather all the information necessary to draw up an accurate map of the Omaha Beach landings. The poor weather conditions—plus some fateful navigation errors—caused more damage than anticipated. To put it simply, no unit reached its exact assigned objective. The fact that each of the targets required specific military equipment, depending on the nature of the enemy defenses, heightened the bloodshed.

Thanks to some naval registers, Getz went on to establish with precision the comings and goings of Robert Capa and other soldiers. Capa stayed on the beach for only an hour and thirty minutes, all told.

To this, Getz added fifteen minutes outbound on the LCVP (Landing Craft, Vehicle, Personnel—Higgins boat) and another fifteen for Capa's return on the medical *LCI-85* (Landing Craft Infantry) to the USS *Chase*, which took him back to England. In other words, two hours in total. Company E, which he'd chosen as escort, was part of the Big Red One: *E* for Easy Company, 2nd Battalion, 16th RCT (regimental combat team). Their objective was in the Easy Red sector. The Higgins boat, drifting on the current, took them farther west, to the Fox Green sector. Thus, Capa didn't land on the beach at Saint-Laurent-sur-Mer, but rather, Colleville-sur-Mer.

To identify the soldier known as the "face in the surf," Professor Getz considered all the active soldiers who were at that precise spot during that window of time. He had to compare the archives with each person's portrait and the information recorded in the photos, which—despite everything—were rich in detail. The number of soldiers in the first wave at 0630 hours was quite limited: 385 men. But still!

In the end, the professor settled on PFC (Private First Class) Huston Riley of the Big Red One, Fox Company, 1st Battalion, 1st Infantry Regiment. Enlisted

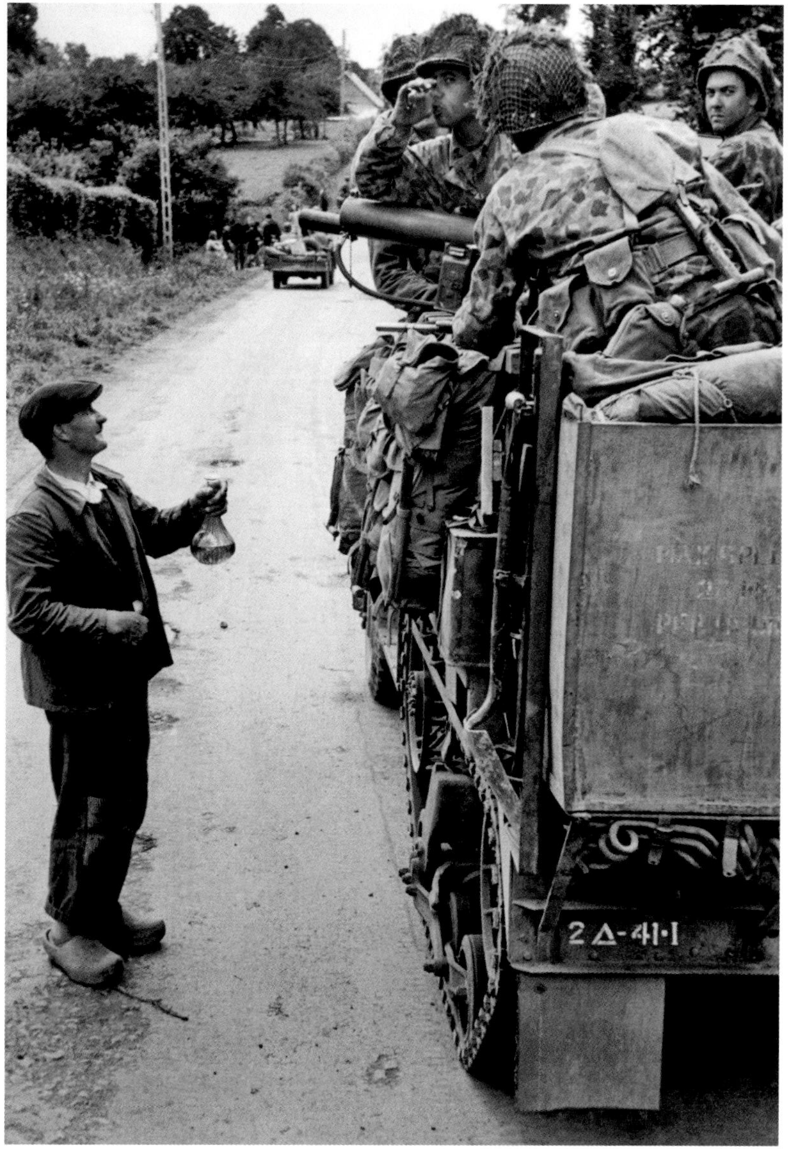
2 Δ-41-I

**Norman farmer offering calvados to American soldiers.
Notre-Dame-de-Cenilly. July 28, 1944.**

voluntarily at the age of twenty, Riley, who bore the regimental number 5760, was a veteran of the North African and Sicilian landings. He'd been twenty-two years old on D-day.

All that was left now was finding him. The biggest surprise for the professor when he went to Hu's house was finding out that not only was Hu still kicking at the age of eighty-six, but that he'd always known he was the man in the famous photo! To Hu Riley, the professor was a nice man with nothing to tell him that he didn't already know.

Hu was a modest man of great kindness. On Omaha Beach, where he'd had so much trouble struggling to his feet in the waves, he'd gotten two bullets in the neck, and later spent two weeks in an English hospital. It was there, in a letter from his mother, that Hu learned he was in a photo in *Life* magazine. His mother had recognized him.

The world press seized upon this beautiful story. The man from Capa's famous photograph of the landing was alive! And this time, they were sure it was him.

In June 1984, on the fortieth anniversary of the landing, *Life* published an interview with another soldier who claimed to be the man in the photo: Edward

Aboard the USS *Samuel Chase*, anchored near Omaha Beach. June 6, 1944.

K. Regan (1923–1998). He based his claim on the fact that he looked a lot like the soldier in the picture, and that he'd been at Omaha. Both of which were true.

Everyone believed this for twenty-seven years. All the more so because Hu, the only one who knew the truth, had never stepped forward. Professor Getz put an end to this error by proving with the archives that Sergeant Regan, a member of the 29th Infantry Division (the famous "Blue and Gray"), had landed on Omaha in the second wave at 0725 hours in the Easy Green sector, approximately 2,600 yards to the west of Capa on Fox Green.

After returning to Omaha Beach in 2004 with his wife, Charlotte, for their sixtieth wedding anniversary, Hu passed away in fall 2011 at the age of ninety. In 2008 the International Center of Photography in New York had invited Hu and his wife to the opening of the exhibit *Capa at Work*. That was where we met him.

"Hu, what's that thing you seem to be pushing in front of you in the photo?"

"My life jacket. I'd just taken it off because when I was wearing it on the beach, I felt like I was sticking out. I figured, the smaller the shape, the smaller the target!"

"Do you remember seeing Robert Capa at Omaha?"

A German general surrendering to American officers in Normandy. June 1944.

"I didn't know who that unarmed guy was. But to be honest, I wondered what the hell a photographer was doing there!"

Though considered among the best pictures of the twentieth century, *The Face in the Surf* never received its due in its day. Robert Capa never won the Pulitzer Prize. In 1944, the jury voted instead for a picture called *The Homecoming*, by an Earle L. Bunker. His photo shows an American Army colonel back from North Africa, hugging his family passionately on a railway platform. Still, a trace of irony remains—a wink, almost, from the Pulitzer jury, no doubt unintentional: this photographer worked for a local Nebraska newspaper called the *Omaha World-Herald*.

BERNARD LEBRUN

Ironing out final details of the landing, aboard the USS *Samuel Chase* off Weymouth, England. Sometime between June 4 and 5, 1944.

OVERLEAF One of the last photos Robert Capa ever took in Indochina: the Mekong Delta, on the road from Nam Dinh to Thai Binh. May 25, 1954, shortly before 3:00 PM.

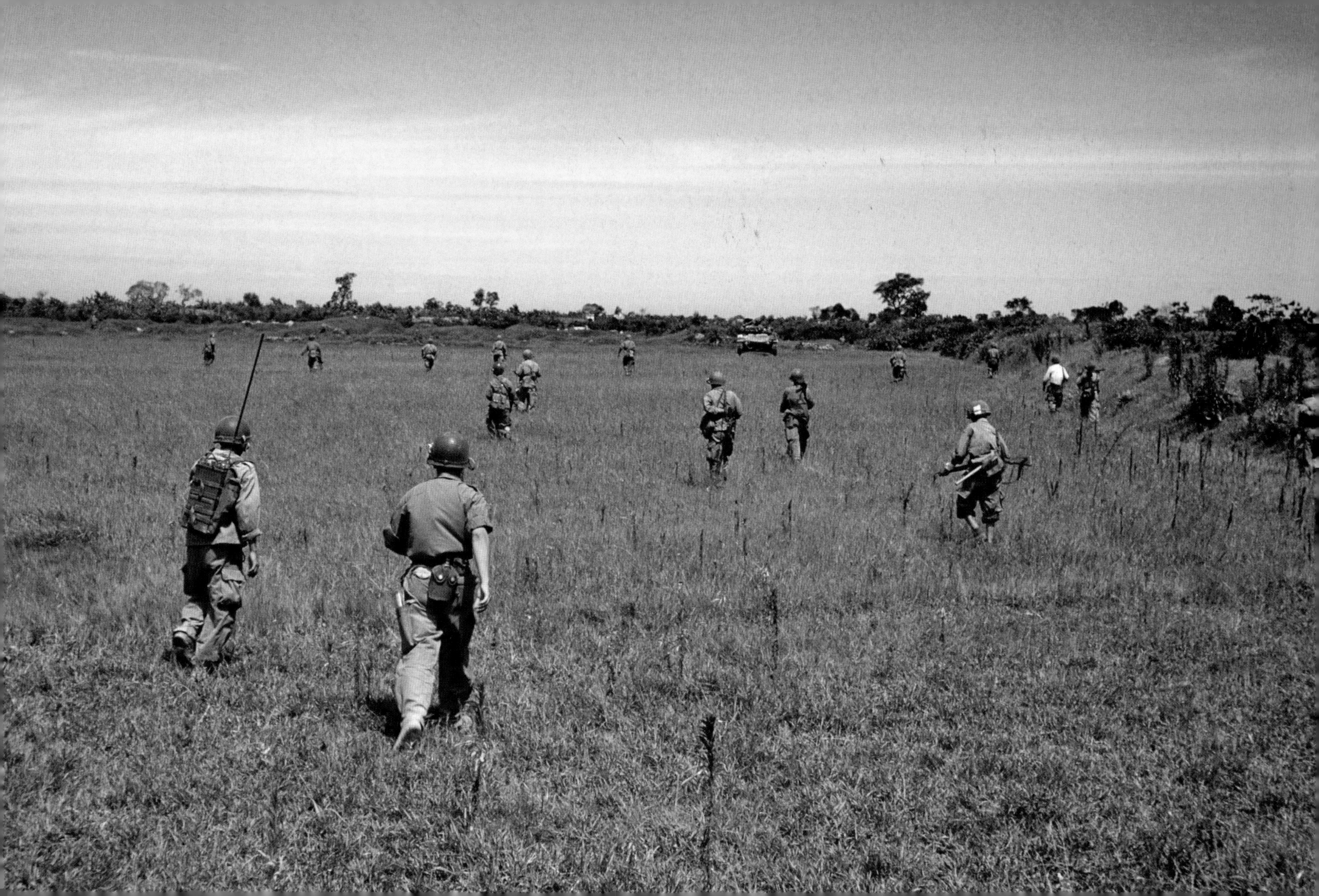

First I'd like to thank the good fortune which helped us complete this account. And then, in order of appearance: YuY, RoC, SéT, CIS, JeCIC, ThT, JoLoB, she, DoB, CyY, EIM, SuM, GaH, BeL, DaC, HaB... And finally thanks to all the Magnum photographers whom I hope will be proud of the trust they placed in us for this series. —Jean-David Morvan

Robert Capa. Photo by Ruth Orkin, Paris, 1953.

Originally published by Dupuis under the title "Magnum Photos - OMAHA BEACH, le 6 juin 1944 - Robert Capa/Morvan+Bertail"
Copyright © Dupuis - Magnum Photos 2014 - www.dupuis.com - all rights reserved.
Based on an original idea by Jean-David Morvan and Clément Saccomani
Story : Jean-David Morvan and Séverine Tréfouël
Drawings and colors : Dominique Bertail
Text : Bernard Lebrun
Graphic design : Philippe Ghielmetti
Published under the direction of Thierry Tinlot.

Special thanks to Cynthia Young and the International Center of Photography.

English translation by Edward Gauvin
English translation copyright © 2015 by First Second
First American edition 2015
English edition book design by Danica Novgorodoff

The following photographs are used with permission:
© Robert Capa © International Center of Photography / Magnum Photos:
cover photo, pp. 58, 59, 60, 61, 62, 63, 64, 65, 66, 67, 69, 70, 71, 72, 73, 74, 75, 76, 77, 78, 79, 80, 81, 82, 83, 84, 85, 86, 87, 88, 89, 90, 91, 93, 94, 95, 96, 97, 98, 99.
© Capa Collection / Magnum Photos: p. 68
© George Rodger / Magnum Photos: p. 92
© Capa Collection / Magnum Photos: p. 100
Courtesy of David E. Scherman © Magnum Collection / Magnum Photos: back cover photo

MAGNUM PHOTOS, 19 rue Hegesippe Moreau, 75018 Paris, France
magnum@magnumphotos.fr / www.magnumphotos.com

Published by First Second
First Second is an imprint of Roaring Brook Press, a division of Holtzbrinck Publishing Holdings Limited Partnership
175 Fifth Avenue, New York, New York 10010
All rights reserved

Library of Congress Control Number: 2015937858

ISBN 978-1-62672-283-5

First Second books may be purchased for business or promotional use. For information on bulk purchases please contact Macmillan Corporate and Premium Sales Department at (800) 221-7945 x5442 or by email at specialmarkets@macmillan.com.

Printed in China by Toppan Leefung Printing Ltd., Dongguan City, Guangdong Province.
10 9 8 7 6 5 4 3 2 1

16 - 0104